POWERHOUSE PRESENTING

Become the Communicator You Were Born to Be

PowerHouse Presenting

Become the Communicator You Were Born to Be

Editor: Susan Snowden, Snowden Editorial Services

Cover art and design: Jane Ware, JB Graphics

Lulu Publishing

Printed in the United States of America

First Edition

ISBN 978-0-6151-5373-5

POWERHOUSE
PRESENTING

Become the Communicator
You Were Born to Be

By Randy Siegel

Table of Contents

Meet Randy Siegel

Randy Siegel is a nationally recognized specialist in professional development, self-branding, communications training, and executive positioning for corporate professional development programs and for individual clients.

"The Career Engineer," Randy Siegel helps organizations build dynamic leaders who make rain, close deals, motivate employees, and are more positive and productive at both work and home. He offers a proprietary process that facilitates self-discovery to clarify personal perspective, true purpose, and professional image. This engaging process transforms high-potential employees into highly motivated and effective leaders who are committed to their organizations and careers. Additionally, it helps presidents and CEOs become more charismatic leaders, spokespeople, and ambassadors for the organizations they serve.

Randy Siegel spent the first half of his career successfully promoting his clients' goods and services. A former executive vice president and partner with Fleishman-Hillard International Communications, Randy opened the company's Atlanta office in 1989 and over the next ten years built it into one of the city's largest public relations firms. During his tenure there, the *Atlanta Business Chronicle* named him one of Atlanta's top marketing-driven public relations executives and "Big Idea Person."

Before joining Fleishman-Hillard, Randy expanded the food division of one of Atlanta's largest independent public relation agencies, A. Brown-Olmstead & Associates. Previously, as director of communications for Canada Dry, he created the company's first communications department. He had earlier worked three years for Atlanta's largest public relations firm, Cohn & Wolfe, where he led the Chick-fil-A, Grolsch Importers, Ford Motor Company, and Milton Bradley account teams. From 1980 to 1983, he served as director of public relations and associate director for the National Kidney Foundation of Georgia. While at the foundation, he helped conceptualize "A Taste of Atlanta," which grew into one of Atlanta's largest fund-raising events.

Now, as a communications trainer, public speaker, coach, and writer, he helps clients market themselves and fast-track their careers. His integration of psychology and sociology with fundamental marketing concepts helps career-oriented men and women become Powerhouse Presenters by forging stronger relationships with key constituents.

Since founding his company in 1999, Randy has conducted hundreds of consultations, presentations, workshops, and coaching sessions for corporations, professional associations, nonprofit organizations, and marketing firms. He has authored professional articles for *Integrated Marketing, PR Journal, PR News, Washington Post, Atlanta Business Chronicle, Atlanta Journal and Constitution, Asheville Citizen-Times, bizlife, Dossier Magazine, MarketingPro.com*, and other publications. His monthly eNewsletter is valued by close to two thousand subscribers worldwide.

Randy's clients include Coca-Cola Enterprises, Earthlink, The Recording Academy (The Grammy Awards), Cox Communications, the Dallas Museum of Art, Viking Range Company, the University of Georgia MBA Program, State Farm Insurance, The Giving Institute, The Honor Society of Phi Kappa Phi, and Fleishman-Hillard International Communications. One client summed up Randy's work this way:

> *You teach far more than communication; your message is about life issues, growth, awareness, and openness. It's powerful stuff, and your ability to communicate it and share your life is inspiring.*

Randy Siegel is a graduate of the University of Georgia Business School with a bachelor of business administration degree in marketing. In his free time, Randy enjoys painting and writing. He and his Dalmatian, Lucy, live in Asheville, North Carolina.

Preface

I have always been a pretty good presenter, but it wasn't until midlife that I became a great presenter. Here's my story. The year was 1995; I was thirty-nine years old, and I was miserable. At first I thought it was my job. I sought the help of an industrial psychiatrist, who after testing me concluded I was in the perfect job. Next, I went to a therapist. Twenty minutes into the session I blurted out that I was gay. I had said it out loud. Pandora's box had been opened. Within a month, I told my wife of fourteen years I was gay. Three weeks later I moved out.

Opening the door to my new apartment, I faced an uncertain future. I had moved from a 3,500-square-foot home to an apartment so small that friends dubbed it the "penalty box." Despite the apartment's modest size, it was a sanctuary. This safe space would become a place for introspection, healing, and growth. It would become an incubator to rebirth my identity, an identity grounded in authentic self.

I continued to see a therapist. Eventually he suggested I join a group therapy session. Reluctantly, I agreed. The first sessions were painful. I couldn't believe that I was stuck in a room for fifty minutes with all these "losers." By the third session, the group had had enough of my attitude. "We have no idea who you are, Randy," they said. "You always seem so perfect. It's impossible to connect with you."

As painful as their words were, they were also precious. I had an epiphany: I would never truly connect with others until I dropped my mask and allowed others to peek behind the curtain of my persona.

Since then, I have learned that nothing makes a presenter more powerful than his or her ability to be authentic. When we drop the illusion of our perfect selves and show people who we are, we connect. They trust us.

Most of us were taught at a young age that it's not okay to be who we are. When we were three or four years old, we began to explore our identity. Like children playing "dress-up" we tried on different personas to see how others reacted to us. During this identity search, most of us became wounded in one of two ways: we were shamed or ignored. To protect ourselves, we adopted a way of being in the world that would garner approval.

I became "the golden boy." Slipping into the armor of perfection, I strived to meet every one of my parents' criteria for being the perfect little boy. It was not until I came out that I was able to get back to the business of being me.

Coming out is not just about sexuality. Straight or gay, there are many closets in which we hide. Coming out is allowing ourselves to be ourselves. It's the process of peeling back layers of tribal conditioning to discover the person we were born to be. Coming out is remembering and celebrating who we are. It's washing the soiled glass of our soul so that glorious light can shine from within.

Since opening my business in 1999 I have coached and trained hundreds of businessmen and women in communications and leadership skills. I also write a popular monthly eNewsletter, and I have published more than seventy articles. Whether speaking, coaching, training, or writing, my message stays the same—it is my motto for living—"Stand in your power by becoming the full expression of all you are."

This message is the overriding purpose of this book. It is intended to remind you that you have the power to become a powerful communicator. It's as simple—and as difficult—as becoming the person you were born to be.

I read once about an ancient Jewish teaching where a young man kneels at the side of his mentor's deathbed. With tears streaming down his eyes, he looks into the fading eyes of his beloved rabbi and asks, "Are you afraid of dying?"

"I only fear when The Holy asks The One Great Question," the wise man weakly answers.

"The One Great Question?"

Slowly, the rabbi raises his head and whispers, "Why weren't you more yourself?"

Presenting can be a wonderful pathway to self-knowledge and acceptance. By sharing who we are, we can become the powerful presenters we were born to be.

Introduction

Some say the secret to being a good presenter is to visualize the audience naked. I say if you really want to be a great speaker, it's the speaker who must strip for the audience.

It's no wonder so many of us are terrified to speak in front of a group. Presenting speaks to our greatest insecurity—what if people don't accept us as we are?

Great speakers and presenters are not afraid to bare their souls to audiences. They strip away their masks and illusions allowing audiences and prospects to see them for who they are. Audiences walk away not only with increased knowledge but with some insight into the presenter as a person.

Whether our goal is to sell, educate, or inform, every speech or presentation has a goal, and the key to reaching that goal is generating trust. In order to trust us, people must know us, like us, and believe we are credible. We have to be authentic.

When we are authentic, we stand in our power. We become the full expression of all we are. We become what I call Powerhouse Presenters. And that is my goal for you: to become a Powerhouse Presenter.

Every professional knows that strong communications skills are critical for their success, but most businesspeople communicate at half-power or less. They may know their stuff, look good, and even make great presentations, but they rarely take the next step: influencing, motivating, and inspiring their audiences.

Powerhouse Presenters do take that step, because they realize the importance of *connection*. They understand that the power to influence, motivate, and inspire entails not simply exchanging information, but actively creating a connection between sender and receiver.

Powerhouse Presenters are clear about who they are and what they stand for, and they boldly communicate this information through their words and actions. By conveying authenticity, authority, vision, conviction, competency, consistency, and caring, they earn trust.

When you become a more confident, competent, and convicted speaker, you can expect to:

- Successfully sell your ideas, products, services, and self;
- Motivate and lead workers;
- Build consensus and encourage teamwork;
- Facilitate problem solving, and
- Build strong relationships with key constituents.

What We'll Cover

I want to help you become a stronger communicator by becoming a more powerful presenter. In the pages that follow, I use three strategies to do so.

Number one, I want to work with you to totally reframe the way you currently think about presentations.

Number two, I hope to show you how to present to people in a way that ensures buy-in throughout your presentation.

Number three, I want to increase your comfort zone with presenting and speaking in public.

We'll begin with the four homework assignments that you must complete before beginning any proposal. Then we'll examine how to put —and hold—presentations together. We'll explore several types of proposals or speeches, including sales presentations, speeches to inform or educate, consulting presentations, and what I call "Snap" presentations for situations in which we are required to think fast on our feet. I will also share some tips for how to look strong when presenting to top management.

Even the strongest presentation can fall apart during the question and answer period. We'll review strategies for any potential challenges during this period.

From here, we'll move into one of my favorite sections: how to present. We'll spend some time on how to make fabulous first impressions. We'll cover visual cues, including dress, stance, eye contact, gestures, and movement. Then we'll move to vocal cues and I will share some common pitfalls I encounter when coaching clients. We'll conclude this section with a discussion of how to manage nerves when you speak, including the proper use of notes and teleprompters.

Powerhouse Presenters earn their audience's attention. I'll review five presentation strategies that will allow you to get audiences to listen and take note. As a bonus, I will cover how to be brief and to the point for those of us who may be a little long-winded. I'll also discuss some specific challenges women may face when presenting. Then I will conclude by reviewing the strongest tool in the Powerhouse Presenting toolbox, authenticity.

Finally, in the resource section at the end of the book, you'll find several additional tools for presenting, including instructions for audio and teleconferencing and Webcasts.

Power Surges

When I opened my training business in 1999, I hired an expert in adult learning. He told me adults put information into one of three buckets:

1. Facts they know, but would like to remember

2. Concepts they may be a little unsure of and need to noodle a bit

3. The great "aha!"

My hope is that you'll experience an aha or two as you read this book. I sure did in writing it. To ensure you don't miss these flashes of insight, I have summarized them at the end of each chapter. I call these summaries "Power Surges." I hope you'll add your own insights to these summaries.

SECTION ONE

HOW TO PUT AND HOLD YOUR PRESENTATION TOGETHER

Chapter 1—Four Homework Assignments

Let's begin with four homework assignments—the four things you must do before every presentation or speech. The first is getting to know your audience. The second is becoming familiar with your venue or where you'll be presenting. The third homework assignment is selecting your visuals, whether PowerPoint or other types of visuals. Assignment number four, and the most important of all the assignments, is getting in the right frame of mind. Here you'll discover how to put yourself in a frame of mind that supports you in being confident, competent, and convicted when in front of an audience.

Homework Assignment One: Know Your Audience

Presenting to strangers is a gamble few successful presenters take. Successful presenters know that analyzing their audience will stack the deck in their favor. Audience analysis begins with interviewing the person I call the information gatherer. In most cases, this is the person who invited you to present. You'll want to quiz this person on the audience's knowledge of the product, program, or service you're presenting, as well as their hot points, roles, and communications styles.

By gauging the audience's understanding of the product or service that you're there to talk about, you'll ensure that you don't preach to the choir or, worse, talk over their heads.

Later in the chapter when we cover the different communications styles, you'll learn how to determine what the hot points of your audience are—or what, I like to say, makes their socks or hose go up and down.

Everyone in the audience has a role. Usually they have one of three roles. First is the information gatherer. Again, that's usually the one who invited you to the presentation. Second is the decision influencer, and third is the decision maker. Before you present, find out who performs what roles, especially the decision maker or makers.

At the beginning of the presentation, you will want to check in on the expectations of your audience. This saved my hide once when I ran a public relations agency. We were calling on a restaurant chain in the South that was considering going public. My financial relations senior vice president had been talking with their chief financial officer (whom we'll call Jim) for months. Finally, he told her, "We're getting ready to pull the trigger on going public, and we'd like to talk to you about public relations support." So we loaded up our six hundred PowerPoint slides, got on the plane, and flew to the city where the chain was headquartered. When we got there we met our contact, Jim, who introduced us to his boss, the chief executive officer (whom we'll call Bob). Since we were meeting Bob for the first time, I began the presentation by saying, "You know, Bob, we spent a lot of time with your chief financial officer, Jim, but we'd like to hear from you. Could you tell us about your expectations and what you hope to get from a public relations firm?"

For the next forty-five minutes, he talked about nothing but marketing concerns. Not once did he mention the company going public. When I asked him about it, he said, "You know, there are some things that we really need to take care of before we go public."

If we'd gone through that entire deck of slides on taking the company public, Bob would likely have been angry at us for wasting his time. Instead, we set aside the PowerPoint presentation and went to what I call a "talking pad," a large pad and easel, and said, "Let's list all your concerns." Together we wrote the proposal over the next hour, and we walked out with a contract. As this tale indicates, it's absolutely imperative that you determine your audience's expectations before you begin, because often they might be different than you thought.

Now let's explore the communications styles. Pay close attention to this section. You'll find this information useful not only for when you present but in almost every major communication in your life, including asking your boss for a raise; dealing with your spouse, boyfriend, or girlfriend; negotiating with a friend; or interviewing for a job.

The Four Communications Styles

First some background. Since ancient times, man has attempted to categorize the different personality styles. In ancient Greece, Hippocrates outlined four temperaments: sanguine, phlegmatic, melancholic, and choleric. Native Americans assigned personality traits to the four directions: east, west, north, and south.

Swiss psychiatrist Carl Jung was the first to scientifically study personality styles. In the 1920s, he published the ground-breaking book *Psychological Types*, in which he identified four behavioral styles: the Sensor, the Intuitor, the Thinker, and the Feeler. Other theories followed and now we have dozens of models from which to choose. My favorites are:

- Myers-Briggs Type Indicator®, created by a mother-daughter team and based on Jung's work

- DISC, which is used almost as much as Myers-Briggs in the business world

- The Birkman Method®, based on the work of Roger Birkman

- CST, or Communicating Styles Technology

- Tony Alessandra's Platinum Rule

- The Enneagram, based upon ancient Sufi wisdom, which explains why we communicate the way we do

I've created my own user-friendly system that borrows elements from all of the above, primarily Tony Alessandra's The Platinum Rule. I've taught people all around the world how to use this system, and they report that it has helped them become stronger communicators both at work and at home.

Let's meet the four communications styles; they are:

- Samuel C. Sensor

- Theodore Thinker

- Ina Intuitor

- Felicia Feeler

You're going to get to know these people intimately. Together, we'll go into their closets and open their drawers. We'll snoop around their offices. We'll discover what makes their socks or hose go up and down, and we'll even peek into their psyches to discover their greatest insecurities.

Before we begin, it's helpful to keep in mind:

- No one style is better than another. Each brings a unique set of skills into the workplace.

- This assessment is based upon self-assessment and as such is subject to bias.

- Research tells us that each of us has all four styles within us, but 80 percent of us have one style we express most of the time, though under stress it might change to another style.

Meet the Styles
Let's meet the four personality styles. Again, they are Samuel C. Sensor, Theodore Thinker, Ina Intuitor, and Felicia Feeler. Even though the names indicate that they are gender specific, they are not. What's more, each has positive and negative attributes, or attributes that are displayed on a good day and others that appear on a bad one.

Exercise: Who Am I?
Let's begin with a quiz. I know you don't have any information yet, but guess which communications style belongs to which name: Samuel C. Sensor, Ina Intuitor, Theodore Thinker, or Felicia Feeler. Place one name in the four empty boxes under Style.

16

Style	Good Day	Bad Day
	• Spontaneous • Persuasive • Empathetic • Probing • Introspective • Draws out feelings of others • Loyal	• Impulsive • Manipulative • Over-personalizes • Sentimental • Postponing • Guilt-ridden • Stirs up conflict • Subjective
	• Accurate communicator • Deliberative • Prudent • Weighs alternatives • Stabilizing • Objective • Rational • Analytical	• Verbose • Indecisive • Overly cautious • Over-analyzes • Unemotional • Controlling
	• Pragmatic • Assertive, directional • Results-oriented • Bases opinions on what he actually sees • Perfection seeking	• Status-seeking • Acts first, then thinks • Lacks trust in others • Nit-picking • Self-involved
	• Original • Imaginative • Creative • Broad-gauged • Charismatic • Idealistic • Ideological	• Unrealistic • Fantasy-bound • Scattered • Devious • Out-of-touch • Impractical

Let's see if you guessed them correctly. The first was Felicia Feeler, the second was Theodore Thinker, the third was Samuel Sensor, and the fourth was Ina Intuitor. How did you do?

Now we're ready to get to know each of the styles intimately. The following tables summarize individual characteristics and communications preferences for each style. As you review each style, see if you can pick out your own. Then try to pick out someone you work with.

Let's begin with Samuel C. Sensor since I know him so well. An ESTJ in Myers-Briggs, I am a classic Samuel C. Sensor. I use the middle initial because Samuel would want it that way. He is all about formality. Above all, he wants you to know his place in the world.

When I conduct classes on the communications styles, students often ask if Samuel will have photographs in his office. I laugh and say, "Only if his family is beautiful."

There's an element of truth in this statement. Status is important to Samuel. Actually, status and productivity. Nothing excites Samuel more than checking things off his or her "to-do list," and that includes interactions with people.

Don't get me wrong. Samuels can be charming. Most are. But if you think about it, you'll feel an air of superiority about them. Samuels have no trouble "standing in their power." They are authoritative people.

Let's take a closer look at Samuel C. Sensor.

Samuel C. Sensor

Areas	Characteristics
Environment	Expresses "status," formal, stiff, somewhat impersonal
Appearance	Formal, loves labels for special occasions. Can be informal, simple, and functional at other times
Demeanor	Impersonal, hurried, impatient, high energy, physically restless, and assertive
Strengths	Administration and leadership
Can be seen as	Unable to see long-range or big picture, impatient, and impulsive
Values/Hot Points	Action, goals, results, wealth, and winning
Goals	Save time, increase productivity
Wants	Control
Biggest Fear	Being taken advantage of
Irritation	Indecision
Under Stress	Dictatorial, insensitive, and impatient
Other Characteristics:	Compartmentalized Lives in here and now Tough negotiator Good at multitasking Learns by doing

Samuel's Communications Preferences	
For decisions, they need	Facts, top-line
Requires you to be	To-the-point, "What can you do for me today?"
Pace	Fast
Level of detail	Top-line
On phone	Succinct
Written word	Bulleted, provide executive summary
Orally	Speaks with conviction
Other Tips:	Confront and challenge. Schedule early meetings. Offer choices. Avoid detail.

Let's meet Theodore next. Theodore Thinkers migrate to analytical careers such as law, engineering, academia, and accounting. They are linear thinkers and excellent students. They can't get enough information, and they love detail.

Theodores seldom give much feedback. They are known for their poker faces. I once gave a workshop to a room full of Theodore Thinkers. The whole time I talked they looked at me sternly with wrinkled brows. At first, I thought they didn't like me or, worse, didn't agree with the material I was presenting. I became more animated trying to win them over. At the end of the four-hour session, I was exhausted. Then it occurred to me, they were Theodore Thinkers; they were thinking. If they had any complaint with me it was that I talked too fast and didn't give them enough time to think about what I was saying.

Meet Theodore Thinker.

Theodore Thinker

Areas	Characteristics
Environment	Expresses "efficiency," tasteful but conventional
Appearance	Formal, functional, conservative, color coordinated but not colorful, under-stated
Demeanor	Impersonal, hard to read, thoughtful, and sometimes considered "dry" or "cold"
Strengths	Planning, problem solving, thinker and doer
Can be seen as	Perfectionistic and critical
Values/Hot Points	Precision, process, procedure – safe choice, ethics
Goals	Justification
Wants	Thoroughness
Biggest Fear	Being embarrassed
Irritation	Unpredictability
Under Stress	Withdrawn, overly cautious (to the point of not being able to make deci-sions)
Other Characteristics:	Resists pressure of any kind Expects you to take initiative Reluctant to give feedback

Theodore's Communications Preferences	
For decisions, they need	Data and documentation
Requires you to be	Detailed, thorough, accurate
Pace	Slow (allow time to think), systematic
Level of detail	Heavy
On phone	Organized, sounds ordered, measured, businesslike, and careful
Written word	Detailed, well-organized, structured, and specific
Orally	Needs time to think
Other Tips:	Plan each meeting carefully. Avoid social talk. Present obvious disadvantages.

When I first opened the Atlanta office of Fleishman-Hillard, I had three employees and one account (Anheuser-Busch's southern business; not a bad account to begin with). I was young and determined. I would not fail. I was so driven that I was an awful boss. Two out of three of the employees quit within the first two weeks. I soon realized that I had a problem with my management skills. I knew that you can't send a duck to eagle school. It would take me awhile to grow into becoming a more empathetic manager. So, I hired a second in command who would complement me. I hired a Felicia Feeler.

Her name was "Julia" and she was the sweetheart of the Atlanta public relations scene; everyone loved her. And with good reason. She was warm, engaging, and truly cared about people.

Julia was a great hire. It was she who created the culture of the office and bolstered morale. Since then, Julia has moved on and now runs her own practice. She still keeps up, however, with most of the original employees. Felicia Feelers are that way.

Felicia Feeler

Areas	Characteristics
Environment	Friendly, comfortable, "homey"
Appearance	Informal, may "costume," dresses for mood more than approval
Demeanor	Friendly, warm
Strengths	Listening and teamwork (often re-sponsible for grapevine)
Can be seen as	Oversensitive and indecisive
Values/Hot Points	Acceptance, feelings, trust, and teamwork
Goals	Stability
Wants	Friendships
Biggest Fear	Sudden change and conflict
Irritation	Insensitivity
Under Stress	Submissive, moody, not concerned with details
Other Characteristics:	Works off of "gut" feelings a lot Can be spontaneous and unstructured Seen as perceptive and insightful Patient

Felicia's Communications Preferences	
For decisions, they need	Personal service and assurances
Requires you to be	Warm
Pace	Slow, relaxed, low pressure
Level of detail	Heavy
On phone	Friendly, chatty
Written word	Warm, brief, and highly personalized
Orally	Warm
Other Tips:	Express enthusiasm; tell why personally important to you. Allow them to get to know you. Schedule meetings around meals. Customize program/individualized approach. Use open-ended questions to draw them out and build trust.

Inas are the ones you want to go have a beer or Margarita with after work. They are great fun. They are charismatic. When I was looking for someone to help sell new business for Fleishman-Hillard, I sought an Ina. Inas are natural salespersons. They are also great big-idea people.

"Dick" (an Ina) and I made a great sales team. Soon we found that the prospect's eyes would lock on one of us—often before we even opened our mouths. The prospect would sense our communication style. If the prospect connected with Dick, I put my ego aside and took notes. Dick then propped his feet on the table and asked the prospect about his golf game. If the eye contact came to me, Dick took notes and I got to the point of our visit. This strategy worked. We began to win more and more business.

Here's Ina Intuitor.

Ina Intuitor

Areas	Characteristics
Environment	"Fun," messy, futuristic
Appearance	Unpredictable, could be fashion forward, flashy, or like "absent-minded professor"
Demeanor	Charismatic
Strengths	Brainstorming and sales
Can be seen as	Scattered, careless, lack of details, "long on vision, short on action"
Values/Hot Points	Big ideas and high energy
Goals	Recognition
Wants	Others' approval
Biggest Fear	Loss of prestige
Irritation	Routine
Under Stress	Sarcastic, impulsive, can become detached
Other Characteristics:	Sees big picture, long-term implications Hates to feel "hemmed in"

Ina's Communications Preferences	
For decisions, they need	How it addresses status/visibility
Requires you to be	Enthusiastic
Pace	Fast
Level of detail	Light
On phone	Playful (jokester)
Written word	Bulleted, writes abstractly
Orally	Dramatic
Other Tips:	Offer testimonials and incentives. Allow lots of time for interaction. Let him/her set the pace. Balance information with stories. Involve as many senses as possible. Save them effort. Involve them in idea generation. Focus on concepts, not on details. Have fun!

Hopefully, you now have a feel for each of the communications styles. Remember, I have given you broad generalizations for each type. Of course, each of us has elements of all four types in us. Did you see yourself? How about someone with whom you work?

Now, see if you can guess the correct style:

If I tend to be empathetic, probing, introspective, and I draw out the feelings of others, who am I?

That's right—Felicia Feeler.

If I'm an accurate communicator, deliberate, objective, and analytical, who am I?

Yes—Theodore Thinker.

If I'm pragmatic, assertive, results oriented, perfection seeking, and status seeking, what personality style am I?

You've got it—Samuel C. Sensor.

If I'm original, imaginative, creative, and charismatic, who am I?

Right again—Ina Intuitor. Of course, all of these positive traits can become negative traits if dialed too high.

It's important to note that this information is intended only to provide a brief overview of the four communications styles. This topic is worthy of a book unto itself. Again, I especially recommend *The Platinum Rule* by Tony Alessandra and Michael J. O'Connor, which inspired much of my model.

Flexing Styles

Most of us go through life communicating with people in ways we like them to communicate with us. For example, I am a Samuel C. Sensor, so my natural tendency is to be on point and to the point. Seldom would I ask personal questions; it takes too much time. There's a better way to communicate, though. By flexing my style to match that of another, I am more likely to get my message across. When I am dealing with a Felicia or Ina, I can flex my style by taking the time to build a relationship before launching into the business at hand. When I am communicating with a Theodore, I can delve into a lot more detail than I would normally; and if I am really on, I might throw in a process or procedure for good measure.

> ### A Tip for Ina Intuitors and Felicia Feelers
>
> You can be somewhat nonlinear in your communications. To get on point and stay on point, I recommend that you use numbers in your speech. For example, "There are three areas I want to address . . . ." Also, when talking to Samuels and Theodores, avoid a lot of small talk. Stick to the topic at hand, and remember that Theodore loves details.

27

"All that is well and good," students often say, "but what do you do when you have a room full of different communications styles?" It's a valid question. Hopefully, you have done your homework, know the communications style of the decision maker and key decision influencers, and have targeted your presentation to them. If you are flying blind, however, I suggest designing the presentation for Samuel C. Sensor (since this style is most often associated with business), and including something, usually a handout with a process, for Theodore Thinker, who is often a major decision influencer. Again, these are broad generalizations. Ina Intuitors and Felicia Feelers are often decision makers and influencers themselves, depending on the industry.

> ### A Tip for Theodore Thinkers and Samuel C. Sensors
>
> Lighten up, guys! Relax and take a minute or two to build some rapport. Get to know Ina and Felicia before launching into your topic. When talking to Ina remember she will respond more to the big picture than to the small details.

It's important to mention that you are not being inauthentic when you flex styles. As explained earlier, each of us has a little of the four styles within us. Merely be aware that you are simply making a conscious effort to intensify the style that matches that of the person with whom you are communicating. The intention is never to manipulate, but to connect. By flexing your style, you are only fertilizing the soil so that communication and connection can grow.

> ### A Word about Pain Avoiders and Pleasure Seekers
>
> In life, we're either pain avoiders or pleasure seekers; our orientation is either to avoid pain or seek pleasure. Generally, Theodore Thinkers and Felicia Feelers are pain avoiders and Samuel C. Sensors and Ina Intuitors are pleasure seekers.

That's it for the four communications styles. I hope you experienced an aha or two. You now know how to research your audience; let's move to your second homework assignment, researching your venue.

Homework Assignment Two: Research Your Venue

In preparing for a presentation you will want to be familiar with the venue, or the space in which the presentation is to take place. Some things you may want to consider include:

- Size of the venue
- Formality of the setting
- Seating arrangement
- Technology options
- Lighting
- Temperature

Whenever possible visit the venue before you present. This is so important that you'll find it in the Power Surge at the end of this chapter. First of all, this gives you an opportunity to visualize yourself in that setting. Secondly, it gives you a chance to check out the culture of the organization, how formal or informal they are. Thirdly, and most importantly, your visit sends the client or prospect a message that you care enough about the presentation to see the venue before presenting in it. Most of your competition will not take this extra step. It will immediately start to distinguish you from those with whom you're competing in the minds of the client or prospect.

If you can't visit the venue beforehand, find out as much about it as possible so you can request how you'd like it set up for your presentation.

For additional support in this area, you'll find the "Speaker's Checklist" especially helpful in the resources section at the end of the book. Now, for homework assignment number three.

Homework Assignment Three: Select Your Visuals

Research says we remember only twenty percent of what we hear, but eighty percent of what we see. Therefore, using visuals in your presentation can help make a lasting impact.

What are the different types of visuals we can use? Some visual formats include:

- Boards
- Flip Charts (Talking Pad)
- Video
- Demonstrations—Show and Tell

And, of course, PowerPoint. Since PowerPoint is used most often by businesses, we'll concentrate our attention on it.

PowerPoint

It is estimated that more than thirty million PowerPoint presentations are delivered worldwide every day. Thirty million!

One survey indicated that the three most annoying things about PowerPoint presentations are:

- The speaker reads the slides to us: 60.4 percent
- The text is so small I couldn't read it: 50.9 percent
- The format is full of sentences instead of bullets: 47.8 percent

Nevertheless, I believe the greatest misuse of PowerPoint is when it is used as a script. PowerPoint should support the message, not become it. Most presenters who use PowerPoint as a script turn their backs on the audience to read the slides, and many aren't even aware they are doing it. First, few things are more deadly to a presentation than reading the audience slides, and second, how can the audience connect with you when they are constantly looking at your back?

Instead, I recommend two underused features of PowerPoint: notes and hidden slides. The notes section of PowerPoint allows you to type notes at the bottom of each slide. Further, PowerPoint lets you hide slides. Thus, the printed slide show can serve as your notes, alleviating the need for the slides to be on view continuously. You can print the deck of slides with the hidden slides and notes, bind it, and place it in front of you. If you have a brain freeze, you can glance down and refresh your memory. Best of all, there is no need to turn your back and read the slides.

During the presentation, the audience's attention should be on you and not the screen. If you use slides only when you need to get across an especially important point and let the screen go to black the rest of the time, you'll keep the audience's attention where it should be.

Many clients are surprised to learn that when they press the "B" key on the computer keyboard, the PowerPoint screen will go to black. When they press the remote forward, the next slide will appear. Use the "B" key whenever there's a lively discussion.

When you do use slides, remember that a slide is like a billboard. You want to get your message to the audience quickly so that they would get it even if they were driving past it at 45 miles per hour. As a result, you'll want to avoid sentences, use bullets, and begin each bullet with an action verb. Never have more than five words per line and three to four lines per slide. And re-

> **Tip: Find the Warm Spot**
>
> Playwright and good friend C. Robert Jones tells me stages have "warm spots." Assuming the lighting is the same, the center of the stage to "stage right" (that is to the audience's left) are the warmest spots of the stage. As a Powerhouse Presenter, you want to position yourself in the middle of the stage or to the audience's left.

member, illustrations such as photos, charts, and graphs carry more visual impact than words.

We want to keep slides up for no longer than one to two minutes, and above all we should remember to communicate only one point per slide. Use a "build" if you have other points to make, but limit moving text. A "build" is when a new bullet or item of information appears on the slide when you press forward on the control. Avoid the temptation to have builds "fly" onto the slide from the top, bottom, right, or left. This can be very distracting.

Other points to remember about PowerPoint slides include:

- Avoid too much text and fancy graphics.

- Practice with the technology you will use during your presentation, as well as with PowerPoint, so that operating it is instinctive and impeccable.

- Round off numbers.

- Use a blue or black background when possible. Stay away from pastels.

- Break from PowerPoint at least every twenty minutes.

- When you show the first visual, ask if everyone can see it.

Finally, two "pearls" to remember about PowerPoint are:

- You may jump to any slide by entering the slide number on the keyboard and pressing "enter."

- Turn off the pointer by pressing Ctrl-L. Press Ctrl-A to bring the pointer back on the screen.

Flip Charts

I call flip charts "talking pads" because they are so interactive. If your decision maker is an Ina Intuitor consider using one. Inas love interaction.

When using a flip chart, remember the four Ts:

1. Touch (Write)

2. Turn (To audience)

3. Target (Establish eye contact with one person)

4. Talk (Begin speaking)

Most of us talk as we write. When we do, our back is to the audience. Instead, I suggest you turn to the flip chart, write in silence, turn back to the audience, connect with an audience member, and begin speaking.

Other tips to remember:

- Leave every other page blank.

- Make sure letters are at least two inches tall, and separate lines by three inches.

- Use color, but use it consistently.

- Use block letters, and only use capitals.

Overheads

Though I have included a section on overheads, I hope you'll never use them. They are dreadfully dull. Nonetheless, if you must use overheads:

1. Limit copy. No more than seven to nine lines of copy per page.

2. Use large type.

3. Bullet; avoid paragraphs and complete sentences.

4. Consider colors and art to increase visual appeal.

5. Use masking tape to frame, or better yet transparency frames that can go in a notebook (prevents pages from sticking together).

6. Position yourself at the projector and not at the screen.

7. Mask by putting the masking sheet under the transparency (the weight will keep it from blowing off at the end and you can read it).

8. Place one transparency over the next to avoid the bright white light in between transparencies.

One Last Note on Visuals

One of the best visuals is a dramatic example. A friend who owns his own public relations agency was making a presentation to a bank. To show the number of newspaper stories he planned to generate in the first three months of work, he dumped three hundred news clippings on the conference room table. He was awarded the account that day.

Homework Assignment Four: Get in the Right Frame of Mind

One of the primary things that distinguishes this book from the myriad of books on presenting is that it addresses the psychological as well as technical components of presenting. I do this because I believe the best presenters work from the inside out. By presenting from the inside out, you present with more competence, confidence, and conviction. You stand in your power.

Stand in Your Power

Sounds pretty good, doesn't it? I don't know of a person who doesn't want to be more competent, confident, and convicted when he or she speaks in public. So where do we begin? Below are four questions to ask yourself before every presentation.

1. **Why am I qualified to present this topic?** If you don't think you're qualified, how effective do you think you're going to be? Find someone more qualified to speak about the topic.

2. **Why am I (how can I be) passionate about this topic?** It's imperative that you're excited about the topic on which you're presenting. Sometimes it's a stretch; sometimes it seems that the only thing I can get excited about is the size of the prospect's retainer. But I always find something—anything—I can get enthusiastic about.

3. **Why should the audience care?** In other words, what's in it for them? Why should they give a darn? What's the benefit they will get from listening to you?

4. **What action do I want them to take?** What do you want them to do as a result of hearing you speak?

Take the time to ask yourself these four questions prior to your presentation, and I guarantee you'll stand stronger in your power when you present.

In addition to the four questions for standing in your power, there are five basic truths about communications. Knowing these can also help you get in the right frame of mind.

Five Basic Truths about Communication

1. All communication is one on one. Whether you are presenting to one person, to ten people, to one hundred people, or to one thousand people, all communication is one to one. Think about it; it's impossible to truly communicate to a room of people. You can only communicate to the individuals in the room. I'll show you how to do this when we talk about eye contact in Chapter 3.

2. All communication is two-way. At my college there were two types of professors: those who engaged the audience and those who lectured. The ones who engaged the students were by far the most popular. We did what we could to avoid those professors who talked *at* us, rather than talk *with* us. Engaging presenters solicit feedback from their audiences. You do this by asking questions and through eye contact. Listen not only with your ears, but with your eyes, watching to ensure that the audience members are getting the message and that you're all on the same page. Also, look into the audience members' eyes as if to say, "Did you get it?" You'll know you're doing this when heads are bobbing up and down in agreement.

3. All communication is "other" focused. Presentations are not performances. In fact, PowerHouse Presenters take the spotlight off themselves and place it on the audience. I have found that most speakers take a narcissistic or altruistic approach to presenting. They either focus on their performance or on the audience.

Narcissistic speakers are performance focused. It is as if they are holding a hand mirror to their faces; instead of seeing the audience, they see only themselves. Such self-scrutiny makes them anxious. They view audiences as judges and react by becoming hyper-focused on their own words and delivery. When they drop the hand mirror and connect with their audience, a different dynamic takes place. They become outwardly focused and communicate in a simple, relaxed manner just like they might when having lunch with an old friend.

There are a number of strategies for shifting our brains from presentation mode to a communications orientation. The two I recommend are (a) involving the audience by asking a question or (b) telling a personal story.

Switching from a narcissistic to an altruistic orientation can be very challenging for some people. The key to making the shift is awareness. Two tools can aid you in becoming more aware. First, you can begin your speech with a question. By inviting audience participation, you trick your brain into thinking that you are in a conversation and not giving a speech. Second, you can tell a story, preferably a personal one. Again, when you tell a story, you trick the mind again into thinking that you are having a conversation.

I was retained to work with one executive on his presentation style. "He is as stiff as board when he presents, but when you are with him socially, he couldn't be more personable," his bosses told me.

We scripted his next presentation to include a question at the beginning of his report. It worked.

By beginning his presentation with a question he engaged his audience and shifted his orientation. He talked *with* his audience, instead of *at* them. When I focus on communication and not the information, I am more relaxed and fluid. I go where my audiences need to go and not necessarily where I had planned.

As a culture we are becoming less adept at connecting with people. I believe that those individuals who are going to be extremely successful in business are going to have the ability to really connect, to understand that connecting is not about them, it's about the others.

4. People respond most to our intentions. If your intention is to "sell" your audience members something, you may fail, but if it's to help them solve a problem, your chances of success are much higher. I read once that people don't care what we know until they know we care about them. Audiences can sense if you're out to help them or to serve your own needs. They also sense if you like them.

What do you think potential clients pay attention to most when they choose one company over another?

- Knowledge of business

- Responsiveness

- I like them.

If you guessed "I like them," you're right. (Next is "responsiveness," and bringing up the rear is "knowledge of business.")

And who do they like? People who like them.

5. People respond less to the actual words we use than to the way we present ourselves. People are as interested in who we are as in what we are presenting. Great presenters let the "you" come through. Which of the following aspects of a presentation have the greatest impact on a presenter's credibility—visual, vocal or verbal (the actual words we use)?

If you answered "visual," you were right.

1. Visual—55 percent

2. Vocal—38 percent

3. Verbal—7 percent

Research shows us that a full 93 percent of our power as presenters is based upon our style (visual and vocal cues), not the words we speak (verbal).

We often forget the difference between communications that are crafted for the eye versus the ear. When we talk for the eye and not the ear, we rely too much on words, sentence structure, even pronunciation, and our communications sound stiff and unnatural.

At first blush, "Paula" appears to be a superior presenter. Every word from her mouth seems perfectly selected, her grammar is flawless, and she always has the "right" thing to say. Yet few would call her a good communicator because few can relate to her. Paula's perfect words form a kind of barrier that blocks people from experiencing the real her.

When I speak I sometimes choose the wrong words and mispronounce the ones I do choose, yet I am considered by most a good communicator. I am successful because I take an altruistic over a narcissistic orientation; I focus not on my performance but on the people with whom I am communicating.

Key to forging strong connections with people is sharing who you are. I read once that before people can follow us, they must have some idea of who we are. This doesn't mean we have to share something that may seem personal, it only means we have to allow people to get a glimpse into our lives. Let me give you an example.

A Theodore Thinker who was head of a major economic organization came to me with the not-so-simple request: "Make me more charismatic." I recommended beginning with a series of 360-degree interviews to gauge his image in the community. The feedback was generally positive: "This guy is incredible." "He is so smart." "He's so competent." "He's such a leader." Only one criticism surfaced: people had a hard time connecting with him because they didn't feel they knew him.

I explained the importance of self-disclosure in creating connection, and I taught him one way to self-disclose without having to share what he considered personal information. I suggested that when he presents, instead of saying, "In a June 28th article in the *New York Times* that reported...," to say, "You know, this morning I was reading the *New York Times* over breakfast, and I saw an article that was really interesting." It's a subtle difference, but one that allows audiences to connect.

Power Surges

- Ask the information gatherer to tell you about the people you will be presenting to. You are especially interested in their roles—decision maker, decision influencer, or information gatherer—and communications styles.

- Remember the four communications styles—Samuel C. Sensor, Theodore Thinker, Ina Intuitor, and Felicia Feeler.

- Flex your style to match that of the decision maker but don't forget the decision influencers.

- Before presenting, check in, and ask your audience about their expectations.

- Whenever possible, visit the venue before you present.

- Visuals help make a lasting impact. Use them.

- You can use PowerPoint but use it sparingly. The attention should be on you, not on the visual. Use the "B" key on your laptop frequently so that the PowerPoint screen is black. When the screen goes to black, the attention will come back to you.

- Talk to the audience and not the screen. Print your slides—along with notes and hidden slides—and bind them. Put them in front of you. Then you'll have no reason to turn around and look at the screen.

- Before every presentation, remember to ask yourself the four questions for standing in your power:

  1. Why am I qualified to present this topic?

  2. Why am I (how can I be) passionate about this topic?

  3. Why should the audience care?

  4. What action do I want them to take?

- Also remember the five basic truths about communications:

  1. All communication is one-on-one.

  2. All communication is two-way.

  3. All communication is other focused.

  4. People respond to our intentions (e.g., how we feel about them).

  5. People respond less to the actual words we use than to the way we present ourselves. In fact, 93 percent of our credibility as speakers is based upon visual and vocal cues.

- The key to forging strong connections with people is sharing who we are.

Chapter 2—Putting It Together

In this chapter you will learn about the different types of presentations that you may be required to give. The first is the sales presentation. Next you'll learn about giving a speech to external or internal audiences. Then we will cover consulting presentations, Snap presenting, and presenting to top management. Finally you will learn how to handle a question and answer session, or Q & A, and how to deal with a difficult audience.

Sales Presentations

There are numerous ways to put together a sales presentation. I will show you one way that I and hundreds of my clients have found particularly effective. It is especially applicable for professional service firms but can be adapted to almost any field or industry.

My system is composed of six elements:

1. Opening

2. Agenda Check

3. Body

4. Summary

5. Q & A

6. Close

And at the end I will offer a bonus step. Even if you don't adopt my system step-by-step, you'll find some pearls of wisdom that can be applied to almost any presentation.

Opening

When giving a presentation to a group of prospects, appoint one person from your team to be "the ringmaster." As the name implies, the ringmaster is responsible for introducing the team and emceeing the presentation. I find it's more effective for the ringmaster to make the introductions, rather than have team members introduce themselves, for two reasons. First, the ringmaster can streamline the introductions so that they don't take too much time, and second, he or she can put each team member in the best possible light without appearing boastful.

When I was the ringmaster, I introduced each team member with a simple formula. First, I gave "the specs" of that person—the name, the title and, when appropriate, the organization. Second, I explained what role each person on the project would play. "Joseph will be your day-to-day contact; Mary will be responsible for financing; and Frank will be responsible for strategy." This helps the prospects begin to visualize each team member in his or her respective role.

Next, I gave only one professional factoid per team member as it applied to their prospect. If we were pitching a computer company, I might say, "I think you'll be particularly interested in the fact that Ted started a small business in college servicing Dell computers." I follow this with one personal factoid, again as it applies to their business. Again, if it was a computer company, I might say, "Ted tells me that he received his first computer when he was four years old." By using this simple process, you'll create a structure that appeals to all four of the communications styles. Samuel Sensor likes it because it moves quickly, and Theodore Thinker approves because it's structured and involves a four-step process. Finally, Ina Intuitor and Felicia Feeler appreciate the process because it shared something personal about each team member.

Next, I'd introduce our firm. Like the introductions, this can become a real quagmire unless managed. In most cases, the prospect already knows a good bit about your firm. After all, they thought enough of you to ask you to present. Instead of sharing all sorts of superfluous information such as when the firm was founded and the number of employees, focus on your firm's unique selling proposition. A unique selling proposition consists of the three things that make your firm, team, product, or service unique—or the three things that separate you from your competitors. Let me give you an example.

During my public relations career, our firm was one of many firms asked to pitch the Georgia Child Care Association. As the ringmaster, I began the presentation with: "You are talking to a slew of agencies. Three things will separate our firm from the rest of the firms you are interviewing. Number one, we're the only agency you will talk to that has its own business-to-business telephone marketing division. We can go into every county in the state of Georgia and recruit one person to run a month-long public service campaign on what constitutes quality child care. No other firm you will talk to today can offer this." (The Samuel C. Sensors and Ina Intuitors took note.)

"Number two, our team is made up entirely of working mothers who are absolutely passionate about your cause." (The Felicia Feelers were ecstatic about this.)

"Number three, we believe enough in your cause, as an agency, that we are willing to donate ten percent of our services pro bono." (Of course, Ina Intuitor loved that; she loves a good incentive. And the Felicias and Samuels responded to our commitment.)

We presented this unique selling proposition three times throughout the presentation: at the beginning, during the close, and later in a follow-up letter to the decision maker. Our strategy worked; we won the account. At our first meeting with the head of the association, she shared, "Randy, we awarded the business to your firm because . . . ," and then she rattled off the three points of our unique selling proposition.

To come up with your unique selling proposition, compare your program, firm, or service with what you believe your competitors offer. Determine what makes you unique, and then craft your messages to appeal to your prospects' communication styles.

After I have introduced the team and offered our unique selling proposition, I provide a teaser that tells the audience members what's in it for them. For example, for a Samuel Sensor, I might say, "We're getting ready to present a proposal to you that will help your business grow by X percent." For a Theodore Thinker it might be: "In our thirty-two years of experience, we've developed a fifty-two-step process for X, Y, Z, and we're going to take you through every step in detail." For Ina Intuitor: "We had the best time putting together the presentation. We brought together a group for a brainstorming session and before we knew it we had more than six hundred ideas written on nineteen sheets taped to the wall. We've selected four of our best ideas, and I can't wait to share them with you." And for Felicia Feeler: "We are convinced that we'll make a great team. To begin with, we believe our culture is very similar to yours . . . ."

Opening recap

- Introductions

    o Your Team

        ▪ Specs (name, title)

        ▪ Role

        ▪ Professional Factoid

        ▪ Personal Factoid

    o Your Firm or Organization

- Three Unique Selling Propositions (presented a minimum of three times)

- What's in it for them? A direct appeal to each of the four communications styles: Samuel Sensor, Theodore Thinker, Ina Intuitor; and Felicia Feeler

Agenda Check

Next comes what I call the agenda check. An agenda check confirms expectations and invites interaction. I suggest four steps to this section:

1. **Distribute agenda.** In it, include the names and titles of the people who are presenting and what you will cover during the presentation. This is the only piece of paper that you should offer the prospect during the presentation. If you provide other handouts or, worse, the written proposal, you may lose your audience members. They will read the handout or proposal rather than listen to you. Additionally, they will read ahead. In fact, most will turn right to the budget.

2. **Ensure it meets their expectations**. Ask if the agenda meets their expectations. Also ask, "Are there any areas you want us to concentrate on? Are there areas we can skip?"

3. **Confirm time**. Confirm how much time you have to give the presentation.

4. **Invite questions**. Invite questions throughout the presentation. You can do so by saying, "We've gained a lot of knowledge about your business over the past few months. We've talked to your branch offices, we've interviewed your people, we conducted research, etc. But we can't pretend to know as much as you do about your business. So as we go through this presentation, tell us what you like. Tell us what you don't like. Tell us if we're on target. Tell us if we're off." That way, you're constantly inviting questions. If there is a concern, you want it out in the open so that it can be discussed. Otherwise, you are unable to defend your position.

Body

I won't go into a great deal of detail on the body of the presentation, other than to say that most have five components. Generally presentations begin with the challenge: "This was the challenge given to us." Next comes the research regarding the challenge, followed by the analysis or implications of that research. Then the proposed solution is offered and, finally, a rationale of the recommendation is presented.

How can you make the body more beautiful? Number one, it should speak to the audience's or prospect's needs. If it doesn't, delete it. Number two, the structure should be simple and logical. Number three, prove the strategy through case studies. Never place the case studies in the back of the proposal out of context.

While presenting the body, check in with the prospect. "Did you see the benefit?" "Does this make sense to you?" "Do you see how this would work for you?" You don't want to move forward until your audience's heads are bobbing up and down like the felt Chihuahua perched on the back window of a pick-up truck.

Body Recap

The body of most presentations includes five components:

1. Challenge

2. Research

3. Analysis/Implications

4. Proposed Solution

5. Rationale

Summary: Restate USP

In the summary restate your unique selling proposition. You might say something like this: "We've just gone through a lot of material. If there's nothing else that you remember, we hope you'll remember this." Then you go back to the three points that distinguish your group from your competition.

Q & A

The proper method for dealing with questions and answers will be covered in detail later in this chapter.

Close

Seminar participants tell me the close is the toughest part of the sales presentation. I would agree. Closing a sales presentation is like asking the prettiest girl in high school out and fearing she'll say no.

Here's a close that doesn't feel so threatening. Try it and see if it'll work for you. "You have a problem, and we agree we have the right solution. The team is in place. When can we get started?"

Plus One

I almost lost a piece of business that later became our agency's largest account (and still is) because I didn't follow this step. The plus one is to keep on selling until the deal is sealed. Continue to stay in touch with the decision maker until she or he has signed the contract. If he's a Samuel Sensor, consider mailing him a case study. If she's an Intuitor, send her some balloons. If she's a Felicia Feeler, take her to lunch; and if he's a Theodore Thinker, send him a case study, a process, or a procedure. Don't become a pest, but continue to stay in touch with the prospect.

Other Tips for Sales Presentations

Before moving on to putting together speeches, let's talk about numbers, seating, and order. How many people should you bring to the presentation? My rule is that you should never outnumber the prospect.

Seating? Ideally, you want to have your ringmaster face to face with their decision maker. You also want to avoid "us versus them seating" with your group on one side of the table and the prospect's team on the other.

Finally, do you want to be the first or last to present if you have a choice? It depends. You want to be first if the prospect already knows about your industry. That way you can set the standard. You want to be last, however, if they know little about the subject. This way you'll have an educated consumer in front of you.

Of course, these are blaring generalizations and depend on individual circumstances.

Speeches

Next you will learn the elements of giving a speech. Entire books are devoted to this subject, so we'll just hit high points here. The best advice for writing a speech is simple: tell them what you are going to tell them, tell them, and then tell them what you told them.

You begin your speech with an opening, which will comprise about 15 percent of your presentation. Then you have the body, which will make up approximately 75 percent of the presentation. Your closing will make up the final 10 percent.

Opening (15 Percent)

The opening is comprised of five components:

1. Grabber

Begin with a grabber to gain the audience member's attention. Here are five different types of grabbers. Tailor your grabber to appeal to the communications styles of your audience.

- Start at the end. Whatever your central point is, bring it up at the very beginning rather than build up to it. For example, if I was asked to write a speech on organ donation I might begin,

"What if I told you that you could turn a senseless tragedy into the gift of life? Would you want to know more?"

- Tell a personal story that backs up the central theme. The personal story should tie back to your central point.

- Use an anecdote, illustration, or analogy.

- Involve the audience. One of the best ways to do so is to ask the audience a question to engage them. You might even ask them to do something physical—stand up, raise their hands, or high-step in place to get the energy moving. But be mindful of the group you're working with. I was once speaking to a group of college administrators and asked them to stand up and reach for the sky. As "Theodore Thinkers," they were resistant. (And that's putting it mildly.) The same tactic, however, was very effective with a group of college students.

- Project into the future or reminisce on the past. For example, "The year was 1955 and ...."

2. Theme/Central Point
In this portion of your speech, you provide the audience with your central point.

3. What's in It for Them
Let the audience know what they might gain from hearing your speech. Remember to:

- Don't tell them; show them. Provide stories and case studies.

- Provide proof.

4. Agenda Check
As you learned with sales presentations, an agenda check is a good way to ensure that the audience members' expectations are in alignment with the material you plan to present.

5. House Rules
When appropriate, go over the house rules, e.g., when breaks will take place, protocol for questions, etc.

Body (75 Percent)

Keep things in units of three whenever possible. Ideally a speech should have no more than three points, and each point should be followed by no more than three sub points. Let me give you an example. Point: "We are changing the way we do business at XYZ Corporation." Sub point 1: "We are changing our personnel policies." Sub point 2: "We are changing our accounting systems." Sub point 3: "We are changing our customer service methods." Whenever possible, provide a story for each sub point to hammer your central point home.

Body Recap

- **Point 1**
  - Sub point 1
  - Sub point 2
  - Sub point 3
- **Point 2**
  - Sub point 1
  - Sub point 2
  - Sub point 3
- **Point 3**
  - Sub point 1
  - Sub point 2
  - Sub point 3

Conclusion (10 Percent)

The conclusion of your presentation should "tell them what you told them" and circle back to the grabber if possible. Your conclusion should include four components:

- Summary of key points
- Call to action with deadline
- List of benefits for taking action by deadline
- Conclude and tie back to grabber

Making Introductions

Earlier in the chapter, we discussed how to introduce yourself during a presentation. Give:

1. Your name, title, department, company or organization

2. Your role regarding their business

3. One factoid about your work experience as it applies to your recommendations

4. One factoid about your personal life that relates to the client's focus or interests

Often clients want to know how to introduce a speaker. Some of the best advice I've seen comes from Dale Carnegie.

Ask the speaker to tell you:

1. Their topic

2. Why they believe their subject is important or of interest to the audience

3. Three specific reasons why the speaker feels he or she is qualified to speak on the subject

Then, follow T-I-S:

T = Topic. Give the exact title of the talk.

I = Importance/Interest. Tell the audience why this topic is important and/or of interest to this particular group.

S = Speaker. Give the audience the speaker's qualifications. Give the speaker's name at the end of the introduction.

Other tips for introducing speakers:

1. Be conversational. Don't memorize. Speak informally.

2. Be brief.

3. Be enthusiastic. Talk with real excitement. Find your own passion.

4. Be warm.

Other Presentations

We'll now cover consulting presentations and Snap presenting. Then we will review several tips for presenting to top management.

Consulting Presentations

A consulting presentation offers our advice or counsel. It's a simple process composed of seven steps.

1. Recap the problem or issue.

2. Explain why the problem exists.

3. Tell what will happen if the problem is not fixed—short term, long term.

4. Recommend solutions.

5. State downside, if any.

6. Offer expected benefits.

7. Present call to action.

My students are often surprised by number five, state the downside. "Why would you poke holes in your own argument?" they ask. I suggest this step for a very important reason: to build trust. By stating the downside, you are letting decision makers know that you have thoroughly researched your recommendations. By admitting that your recommendations are not without risk, you are presenting the entire picture so that they can make a more informed decision.

Snap Presenting

Some people are naturally good on their feet. If asked to speak extemporaneously, they can wax on elegantly. Unfortunately, I am not one of them. Dale Carnegie offers some excellent advice for those of us who need a little help when asked to speak off the cuff. He suggests that you give an example or story about the issue at hand. Then present the central point. Next tell what action you want the audience to take. Finally end with the benefit to them for taking the action (unless they're pain avoiders; then you'll want to outline the negative consequences for not taking the proposed action).

Here's an example:

Story: *Two weeks ago, Bob Ranison resigned. Even though he was with our firm for twelve years, chances are you don't know him. Bob is a star and now he is going to be one of our competitors. With him he takes an in-depth knowledge of our strengths as well as our weaknesses, and it will cost us more than twenty-five thousand dollars in hard costs and lost productivity to replace him.*

Point: *Bob is not leaving for more money or better benefits; he is leaving because he is no longer challenged with us.*

Action: *We can no longer afford to create career tracks for only top management. We need to identify high potential employees throughout the organization and develop a career track for each of them.*

Benefit: *If we do this we can ensure that more "Bobs" don't leave us and that we'll retain our best and brightest employees.*

Snap Recap
1. Example

2. Point

3. Action

4. Benefit

Presenting to Top Management
Participants in my training sessions often ask if I can give them some tips for presenting to top management. I offer five:

1. Get to the point and stay on point.

2. Don't preach to the choir.

3. Interpret the facts. Convey meaning not information.

4. Share the bad news first.

5. Use graphs to tell the good news and tables to tell the bad. (Think about it: A graph is usually more dramatic than a table.)

So far we've discussed how to put powerful presentations together. Now let's turn our attention to how to hold them together. Even the strongest presentations can fall apart during the question and answer period and when audiences take control of the presentation. Here we'll review how to handle questions and answers and how to balance giving the audience what they want with ensuring you get your message across.

Questions and Answers (Q & A)

Even if you invite questions and answers throughout, you're still going to have someone, usually Theodore Thinker, who is going to wait until the very end to ask questions. It's a good idea to allow at least 10 percent of your time for Q & A.

When I was in public relations, we used an expression when training people to be spokespeople with the media that applies to Q & A. It says: "Dread it, get it." It means if you dread a question, chances are you'll be asked it. One of the most important five minutes you can spend preparing for a presentation is to brainstorm with your team and decide on the worst possible question the prospect could ask you. Then prepare a response.

When working with people to become stronger spokespeople during media interviews, I teach $Q = A + 1$. This same formula works equally well for presenting and speaking. It means Question = Answer plus one Unique Selling Proposition. When asked a question, respond succinctly; then deliver a unique selling proposition.

Sometimes there are no questions. Dead silence. In this case, the group may need a little warming up. One strategy is to throw yourself a soft pitch and then hit the ball out of the ballpark. Ask yourself a question: "You know, many times, prospective clients ask me . . . ." The question I ask myself is an easy one, and my response includes our unique selling proposition.

Whenever possible, give an example or tell a story as a part of your answer. I often recommend that clients weave case studies into their answers during Q & A. Finally, if a person appears perplexed after your answer, you may want to inquire if you answered their question. Often you'll find they asked the wrong question. He or she may say, "What I meant to ask you was . . . ."

Never interrupt someone who is asking a question. Avoid becoming defensive. Finally, watch your body language. Sometimes when asked a difficult question, we step back. We may not even be aware of it.

Stepping back gives the message that we are retreating in the face of challenge. Instead, stand your ground and, depending on your audience, step toward the questioner.

Q & A Recap

1. Allow 10 percent for Q & A.

2. Dread it, get it.

3. Q = A + 1

4. Ask yourself the first question.

5. Provide examples.

6. Don't interrupt or be defensive.

7. "Did I answer your question?"

8. Step toward, not back.

Balancing What the Audience Wants With Delivering Your Message

I love it when audiences become excited about the material I am presenting. Sometimes they get so fired up that they get stuck on one aspect of the presentation, and the presentation comes to a halt. When this happens, I remember to be "other focused." I give them the option: "You know, it looks like we've got a lot of energy around this discussion. I still have a number of other topics to share with you. Do you want to continue to discuss this or do you want to move ahead?" Usually, when you give them this option, they'll move ahead. Sometimes you have no choice; you have to move on. In these cases, I might say, "I hate to stop this great discussion, but in the interest of time I need to move us on."

There will be times when an audience member, most likely an Ina Intuitor, will start "grandstanding." This person may try to take over by asking lots of questions, sharing personal experiences, or talking about something that may not be relevant to the topic at hand. Look around the room to see how the other audience members are reacting to that person. If they are put out, which in many cases they might be, then consider placing the grandstander in the "parking lot." "Gosh, Trey, this is really a great discussion, but in the interest of time, I'm going to move forward. However, I'd like to talk to you more about that after the presentation." Then, jump right into the presentation. You've allowed Trey an opportunity to save face, and you've taken back control of the presentation.

Sometimes humor helps when you are in a tight spot. If you find yourself doing some verbal sparring with an audience member, you may look to the group and say something light-hearted like, "You didn't know you were coming to a boxing match did you?" By recognizing the situation, and making light of it, you can ease any mounting tension. Above all, keep your composure!

Power Surges

- A particularly effective system for putting together an external or sales presentation involves six—plus one—elements:

  1. Opening

  2. Agenda Check

  3. Body

  4. Summary

  5. Q & A

  6. Close

- Plus One: Keep on selling until the deal is sealed!

- The only material that should be distributed before or during the presentation is the agenda.

- Never outnumber the prospect during a presentation.

- Avoid "us versus them" seating.

- Check in with your audience to ensure they are on board. "Does this make sense?" "Do you see how this could work for you?"

- In writing a speech, remember this simple advice: "Tell 'em what you're going to tell 'em. Then tell 'em, and finally tell 'em what you told 'em."

- There are seven steps to writing a consulting presentation:

  1. Recap the problem or issue.

  2. Explain why the problem exists.

  3. Tell what will happen if the problem is not fixed—short and long term.

  4. Recommend solutions.

  5. State the downside, if any.

  6. Offer expected benefits.

  7. Present a call to action.

- If you are asked to present on your feet, remember Dale Carnegie's suggested format:

  1. Example

  2. Point

  3. Action

  4. Benefit

- When presenting to top management, interpret the facts. Convey meaning, not information. Also, use graphics to tell the good news and tables to tell the bad.

- One of the best ways to use five minutes of preparation is to consider this: What is the worst question you might be asked, and what will your response be?

- Q & A is an excellent time to provide case studies and deliver your unique selling propositions.

- If the group becomes stuck on one topic, give them the option of continuing the conversation or moving on. "It looks like we have a lot of energy around this topic. I still have a number of topics to share with you. Would you like to continue the conversation or move on?" In most cases, the group will opt to move on.

- Consider placing grandstanders in the "parking lot."

SECTION 2

HOW TO DELIVER A PRESENTATION

Chapter 3—The Ninety-Three Percent Solution: Visual and Vocal Cues

The Four-Second Window

In the first chapter you learned about the four homework assignments—getting to know your audience, becoming familiar with your venue, selecting your visuals, and getting in the right frame of mind. In the second chapter you became familiar with the different types of presentations you may be required to give—the sales presentation, giving a speech, consulting presentations, and Snap presenting. Now we are ready to cover one of my favorite topics: visual and vocal cues.

Have you ever been on a blind date? Come on, admit it. Sure you have. Let's say your date is coming to your home to pick you up. The doorbell rings. What's the first thing you do? You look through the peephole. Snap! In the time it takes a camera to snap a photo, you formed an impression, and your poor blind date didn't even have a chance to open his or her mouth.

Okay, some of you won't 'fess up to ever having been on a blind date—or it's been so long you've forgotten. So I'll give another example. Let's say you're interviewing someone for a job in your organization. You walk out into the lobby, you extend your hand, and within seconds you know whether or not you are going to hire this person. You haven't even seen his or her resume. But you already know. I call this the four-second window.

Research tells us that within four seconds we form assumptions about the person we're meeting. In fact, scientists recently discovered that when we meet someone new, our mind processes more than one hundred messages a second regarding that person on a subconscious level.

We do it not only to other people; other people do it to us. So it becomes imperative to know how to make impressive first impressions. What we say rarely creates first impressions; in most cases it's the way we look and our vocal quality. As we learned in Chapter Three, 93 percent of our credibility as a speaker is made up of visual and vocal cues, and since visual cues account for 55 percent of that 93 percent, we'll start there.

Visual Cues

Within four seconds most of us form an immediate judgment and then we spend the next thirty minutes justifying our original response. What's so interesting is that nine out of ten times, our first impression is spot-on.

For some, this "four-second window" is a breeze. These rare men and women have naturally high "likeability factors" —a face, smile, or presence that people find instantly attractive. I call these faces "juicy faces." Juicy faces are open, inviting, and warm. Looking into them, we feel comfortable. Most of us, however, are not blessed with a juicy face. We have to earn a positive likeability rating.

When we present, five factors contribute to first impressions: dress and grooming, stance, eye contact, gestures, and movement. We'll look at each.

Dress to Impress

When I ask workshop participants to name three components of professional image, their first response is almost always dress. Clothes may not make the businessperson, but clothes *do* create first impressions that can make or break careers. I suggest that clients think of their clothes as a communications choice. "What do you want to communicate?" I ask.

Experts abound on the subject of proper dress and grooming while presenting, yet the best advice I found came from one of my seminar participants. She suggested looking into the mirror and noticing if anything stands out; if it does, take it off or change it. We want the audience's attention on our face. This means avoiding dangly earrings (they move and catch light), distracting hair such as bangs that get into our eyes, an art pin, or a brightly colored scarf or tie.

One man I coached loved loud ties. While his neckwear reflected his outgoing personality, it also distracted from his presentation. The audience focused on his ties rather than his face, missing much of what he had to say.

Here are some other tips on how to dress to impress.

For Both Businesswomen and Men

1. Pay particular attention to your shoes. Believe it or not, they are often the first thing that people notice about us. Few things create worse impressions than scuffed or poorly maintained shoes.

2. Almost as important as the clothes you wear are the way they fit. Find a seamstress or tailor you trust. Few things will destroy your credibility faster than an ill-fitting suit, shirt, or blouse. I worked with a man who was a terrific presenter yet his tight shirts (he was a little overweight) made him appear sloppy and not prepared. He began receiving positive feedback on his presentation skills once he began wearing larger shirts. (Brooks Brothers offers a wonderful shirt with a full cut.)

3. Take good care of your clothes. Make sure they are dry-cleaned and pressed.

4. Avoid colognes or perfumes in the workplace. (Even on a date, you should have to "hunt" to discover scent. Think of it as a treasure hunt.)

5. Get in shape. Research shows that those who are in good physical shape demand higher credibility and authority. If you are overweight or underweight, look for clothes that flatter and that don't accentuate problem areas.

6. Smile often. Consider whitening your teeth. This process is easy and inexpensive these days.

7. Own at least one suit that you have deemed your "power suit." Wear it when you could use a burst of confidence such as for an important presentation, job interview, or performance review. Mine is a black Armani, and I feel fabulous in it.

8. Do not dress casually for a job interview or promotion, no matter how casual a prospective company's office environment may appear. Remember to dress one step up from your prospect.

9. Look around the office and see how your bosses are dressed. Find role models who are company stars.

For Businesswomen
1. Skirt length should be just above the knee, to the knee, or slightly below. Skirts that come to the ankle are appropriate only when they are in style. Often women ask me about pants; pants are acceptable in the workplace. In fact, I like them.

2. Jackets add authority; suits add even more authority. Avoid wearing dresses when authority is important to you.

3. Blouses should be cotton or silk and should be white, or some other light color.

4. Select suit colors that make you look and feel attractive. If you are unsure what those are, consult with a color expert. It could be one of the best investments you make on your wardrobe.

5. Match shoes to your outfits. Avoid open-toed shoes and very high heels. Both rob authority.

6. Keep jewelry simple. Avoid multiple earrings, rings, and bracelets.

7. As you approach your forties and fifties, your facial coloring may change. Consult a makeup expert and consider coloring your hair. Makeup and hair color should be soft and natural.

8. Save cutesy (those Santa Claus sweaters), sexy (miniskirts and low-cut or see-through blouses), and flashy clothes (sequins) for your off hours.

9. Opt for a briefcase rather than a purse.

10. Pay attention to your nails. Get a manicure. Long nails belong on the silver screen not in the office.

For Businessmen

1. Your power suit should be navy. This is a classic. Wear it with a white shirt. Gray suits are an ideal second choice, as is a blue oxford cloth shirt.

2. Avoid excessive jewelry. One ring and a watch. Save bracelets, chains, and flashy cufflinks for the weekend.

3. A wing-collared shirt is considered more formal than a buttoned-down shirt.

4. Sport a contemporary, conservative hairstyle without gels. Rarely have I seen a man with dyed hair who didn't look like he dyed his hair.

5. Most experts say your socks should match your suit or slacks. I tend to wear black socks almost always for work. (They are easier to match.) So far, I haven't been busted.

6. Researchers have reported that more than 70 percent of interviewers and top management do not approve of heavy facial hair. Shave every day.

7. Business casual should be dress pants or khakis, no jeans. Wear a collared shirt. Keep a blazer at work in case an unexpected event pops up. A navy blue blazer will give you increased authority.

8. Avoid garish, themed, or cutesy ties. Purchase only silk ties.

9. Watch your grooming. Trim your nails and make sure they are clean. Trim nose and ear hair.

10. Your belt should match the color and finish of your shoes. For example, shiny black shoes require a shiny black belt. On the average you will want to purchase a belt that is a size larger than your waist. Keep buckles simple.

In addition to dress, four other factors contribute to first impressions: stance, gestures, movement, and eye contact.

```
┌┄┄┄┄┄┄┄┄┄┄┄┄┄┄┄┄┄┄┄┄┄┄┄┄┄┄┄┄┄┄┄┄┄┄┄┄┄┄┄┄┄┄┄┐
```

Dress One Step Up from Your Audience

While training a group of polo shirt and flip-flop clad high-tech executives in communication skills, I once was dressed authoritatively in a dark suit and silk tie. When I got to the part of my presentation on dress, they challenged me.

"Practice what you preach!" they teased. When I asked them what they meant, they explained that rather than one step up, I was dressed a staircase away from them. "You are hard to identify with," they said, and they were right. The next day, I showed up in khaki pants, a blue blazer, and a button-down shirt. Once again, the students had taught the teacher.

```
└┄┄┄┄┄┄┄┄┄┄┄┄┄┄┄┄┄┄┄┄┄┄┄┄┄┄┄┄┄┄┄┄┄┄┄┄┄┄┄┄┄┄┄┘
```

Stance

How we hold ourselves speaks volumes about how we feel about ourselves. Do you remember those girls in high school that were not so pretty, but still popular? By being poised and perfecting their posture, they conveyed such confidence that they appeared far more physically beautiful than they were.

When we present, the way we stand conveys the authority we exude. Like appearance, stance contributes to instant credibility.

For many women, stance is a challenge. Most women are taught at a young age to assume a dancer's pose, feet close together with one toe pointed out at a 90-degree angle. While this stance may be feminine and pretty, it holds no authority.

Instead, I counsel both men and women, to stand tall, feet shoulder width and pointed outward, with weight evenly distributed. Knees should be slightly bent to act as a shock absorber should your knees shake when you are nervous. While it is important to gesture naturally, hands should drop to the sides when not in use.

Stance is imperative in establishing credibility so don't hide it. At no time should speakers stand behind a podium, desk, table, or other obstacle. Great speakers allow their audiences to see all of them. It's as if the speaker is sending the message, "Look, here's all of me; I have nothing to hide. You can trust me." Audiences must see, trust, and connect with us in order to be persuaded by our message.

Eye Contact

The eyes have been called the "windows of the soul." As such, they are one of our greatest tools in winning audiences.

I coach executives to begin each presentation by standing in silence, finding a friendly face, establishing eye contact, taking a deep breath, finding another friendly face, and then beginning their talk. This process can seem like it takes a lifetime (our sense of time is often distorted when we speak), but it takes less than ten seconds and it helps speakers become grounded and begin their presentations with authority. But of all the advice I could give on eye contact, nothing is as important as giving "one thought per person."

One Thought per Person

If you took a speech class in high school or college, perhaps you remember what your professors told you about eye contact. Most professors suggest moving our heads around the room and delivering short blasts of words to audience members, like a sprinkler head. Others recommend blankly staring at the exit sign at the back of the room—or, worse, at someone's forehead. (Pity the poor recipient of such eye contact. Most would flee in terror to the closest mirror to see if a new zit has popped up.) They say these tactics will help you avoid losing your place. Wrong. The richest form of eye contact is when we establish eye contact with one person and deliver one thought per person. That thought does not have to be a paragraph. A simple sentence or even sentence fragment will do. For example:

First Person: "I am going to present to you three topics."

Second Person: "The first is X."

Third Person: "The second is Y."

Fourth Person: "And the third is Z."

Fifth Person: "Let's look at each in some detail."

And when you communicate that one thought per person, connect with each person as if he or she is the only person in the room. "Visualize a dark room with a single pen light on that person. You can't see anyone else in that room except for the person with whom you're communicating," I instruct clients during coaching sessions.

Confidence is in the Eyes

One study showed that speakers who were ranked "sincere" looked at their audiences an average of three times longer than those who were rated "insincere." Yet researchers tell us most people make eye contact only 45 to 65 percent of the time.

I know a brilliant businessman who rarely looks people in the eye. I can only assume that he is socially awkward. I have noticed, however, that his eye contact improves when he's talking about something he is passionate about.

Eye contact can be directly correlated to one's confidence. The more eye contact we engage in, the more confident we appear. Intensive eye contact can be uncomfortable for both the presenter and audience members, but it's also highly effective in holding the audience's attention.

Gestures

Many clients ask about gesturing. "Your gestures are like your thumbprint: each person's gestures are different," I teach. I wouldn't presume to tell you how to gesture any more than I would tell you what you should eat or when to go to bed, but I will warn you against a few gestures that leak authority.

Choir Boy or Girl: Men and women can look like little choir boys or girls when they hold their hands up by their chests. Unfortunately, many of us make this angelic pose "home base," which restricts our volume. Instead, I suggest that clients drop their arms to their sides when they are not gesturing.

Happy Pockets: I once worked with a senior vice president who jingled the change in his pockets as he presented. His voice was so soft that we could barely hear it over the rattle from his pockets. I finally took the coins from his pockets before he presented. Unfortunately, he still kept one hand in his pocket, again leaking authority, but at least we could hear him.

Firing Squad and Ten Hut!: Some presenters put their hands behind their backs and stand stiffly as if standing in front of a firing squad. Others—especially those who self-consciously take my advice of dropping their arms to their sides when not gesturing—place their arms stiffly to their sides like wooden soldiers. Ten Hut! Neither is effective. Again, we should gesture naturally, and when we are not using our hands, drop our arms by our sides.

Fig Leaf: Men presenting to powerful women frequently use this gesture, placing their hand over their private parts as if protecting themselves.

Bear Hug: In a bear hug, we embrace ourselves. When we cross our arms this way we give the message that we are closed.

Lady Macbeth: I often employ the "Lady Macbeth"; I rub my hands as if I were washing blood off of them. This can appear a little creepy. It's not a very effective gesture if you are trying to win people over to your side, is it?

Some of us are hand-talkers; we use our hands a lot when we speak. If you are a hand-talker, that's okay, but when you're finished with your hands, drop them. Otherwise, you may restrict your vocal capacity.

The face has eighty facial muscles capable of seven thousand facial expressions. It's imperative that your facial expression match the message. I once worked for the National Kidney Foundation of Georgia, and I traveled around the state talking about organ donation. When I saw a videotape of myself giving my talk, I was horrified. As I said, "When your loved one dies…" I was smiling. Ugh. This was a hard habit to break. I finally got a friend to join the audience as my "spotter." Every time I smiled inappropriately, he would raise his hand alerting me to the fact that I needed to lose the smile.

On the other hand, the most important of facial expressions is the smile. Pianist and comedian Victor Borge once described a smile as the "shortest distance between two people."

Movement

"Is it okay to move when we talk?" one seminar participant asked. When we are nervous, our nervous energy has to go somewhere. For some of us it goes to our feet, causing us to pace or rock back and forth. Constant movement becomes distracting for the audience.

When we anchor our feet—especially when we first start speaking— this energy will travel up our legs and manifest itself in facial expression, and it is our faces—even more than our words—that capture and captivate audiences. So limit your movement, especially at the beginning of your speech.

If you must move, deliver one thought to a person; then in silence walk, stop, plant, lock eyes with an audience member, and then deliver a thought to that person. Do not talk and walk. It's almost impossible to maintain eye contact.

Vocal Cues

Remember that 55 percent of what audience members initially think of you comes from your personal appearance. And a full 38 percent of their first impression is based on the sound of your voice.

When I ask seminar participants for attributes of vocal quality, they almost always respond with:

- Pitch

- Speed/rate

- Projection

- Articulation

- Breath

- Accent

I am often asked about accents. The most important thing we can do if we have a heavy regional or foreign accent is to diffuse interest by addressing it early in the presentation. I worked with a woman with a beautiful English accent, but her accent was so intriguing that audiences found themselves listening to it, rather than to her message. She learned to diffuse interest by making a little joke at the beginning of each presentation. "You may be wondering about my accent," she would begin. "Many people want to know where I'm from. Well, I will tell you...I'm from South Georgia." After a good laugh, the audience could concentrate on her message.

I also worked with a man who stuttered. Again, we found when he was up front with folks they could relax and listen to his message. He began most presentations by smiling and saying that he might stutter a little, and if he does to please stick with him.

Have you ever heard your voice on a tape recorder or answering machine? Many of us do not like the sound of our voice. Perhaps you believe your accent is too strong, you speak too slowly, or your voice is too melodious. Actually very few such vocal challenges concern me unless they hinder the speaker from making his or her point. Here are the more common pitfalls I run across in my work.

Common Vocal Pitfalls and Their Antidotes

Rapid-fire Fiona. Research shows that most listeners prefer speakers whose rate of speech matches their own. Still, some of us talk so fast that it is sounds like we deleted all punctuation from our speech. Without commons, periods, semicolons, and colons to stop us our speech becomes one run-on sentence. If we think of words as water, it is as if a tidal wave washes over the audience so fast that none of the speaker's thoughts soak in.

Rapid-fire speakers can slow down their speech rate by looking for the commas, periods, and other punctuation marks and pausing, adopting the "one thought per person" rule, and frequently checking in with audiences. For those with more advanced cases of rapid fire, I suggest scripting pauses into their speech.

Tiny Tom. The Tiny Tom voice is especially prevalent among women. Taught at an early age that is it unappealing for women to be loud, many lower the volume of their voices. Speaking softly can fracture authority. Further, research shows us that the higher the pitch of the voice, the less credibility it carries. I recommend that Tiny Toms increase their volume, lower their pitch (if possible), own their space by standing tall and wide, and connect with their authority by asking the four questions for standing in your power (see page 30).

Interestingly, if a person has an imposing presence, speaking softly can also give the impression of being in control. I worked with a man who was six feet, seven inches tall. He towered over most people. He spoke very softly, and in his case this strategy worked for him. We leaned in to hear every word. He had us in the palm of his hand.

Monotone Mike. Some men, and fewer women, leak authority by speaking in a monotone. Audiences find it hard to stay focused on a speaker whose voice lacks passion and conviction. Effective strategies for Monotone Mikes include increasing their volume, owning their space, and connecting with their authority. In addition, varying facial expressions naturally changes volume and pitch.

Up-talking Tina. Up-talking Tinas are like stereotypical Valley Girls. They have an upward inflection at the end of every sentence that makes statements sound like questions. Comedian Jerry Seinfeld called them "up-talkers." This manner of speaking totally destroys authority and credibility because the speaker doesn't sound convicted about his or her topic. Most people who are Up-talking Tinas don't know it. Once identified, the best way to effect change is to be aware of the problem. Team with a "spotter" who can point out when you are speaking this way, and exaggerate this mannerism in order to hear it for yourself.

Verbal Junk Jim. Verbal Jim may use a lot of ums and ahs or he may over-use superlatives or phrases such as "super" or "you know" or "basically." All of us use these, of course. But when they start to get distracting, is it time to take note. Probably the best way to reduce the amount of verbal junk is to recruit a spotter who will bring it into your consciousness.

A while back, I was conducting a PowerHouse Presenting workshop for a group of credit union officials when an outspoken participant pointed out that I had used "Does that make sense?" no less than thirty-two times in a two-hour period. I had no idea. I was a little embarrassed, but I was also grateful. I am now very careful to limit this phrase.

Breathless Brenda. Breathless Brendas forget to take time to breathe, so they are gasping for air by the end of a paragraph. Breathless Brenda must identify the commas, periods, and other punctuation in their presentations, and use them as opportunities to take a breath. In fact, many of the antidotes for Rapid-fire Fionas work equally well for Breathless Brendas.

Cracklin' Rosie. These presenters have a voice that cracks. To help keep your voice from cracking, warm up by humming a few bars of a song (if you are alone). I often sing with the radio on my way to a seminar.

By the way, if you mumble or consistently get tripped up on words, your tongue may be getting jumbled up with your lips and teeth when you talk. You can improve your enunciation by placing the tip of your tongue in back of your front teeth and then flicking it back in your mouth. Do this as fast as you can for a few minutes each day.

With practice, most presenters can use their voices to convey passion, conviction, intelligence, and warmth.

Three Tips for Good Vocal Hygiene
1. Don't smoke, yell, or strain your voice.

2. Keep lubricating mucus flowing smoothly by drinking eight to ten glasses of water a day. (When you drink sufficient quantities of water, your urine should be pale.)

3. Avoid phlegm-producing foods/beverages including dairy, fried or oily food, mayonnaise, or mints. (Mints can dry out your mouth.)

Again, for most people vocal quality is not a major concern. Speak about something you believe in and the chances are your vocal quality will be at its best. Of all the advice I have ever read on vocal quality the best comes from nineteenth century philosopher Elbert Hubbard:

The best way to cultivate the voice is to not think about it.

Actions become regal only when they are unconscious; the voice that convinces, that holds us captive, that leads and lures us on, is used by its owner unconsciously.

Fix your mind on the thought, and the voice will follow. If the voice is allowed to come naturally, easily, and gently, it will take on every tint and emotion of the mind.

The Power of the Pause

Psychologists say a typical group will withstand about fifteen seconds of silence before someone breaks the silence and speaks. There is tension in silence yet power in the pause.

"The right words may be effective," said Mark Twain, "but no word was ever as effective as a rightly timed pause."

One of the greatest piano virtuosos of the twentieth century, Arturo Rubinstein, was once asked by an ardent admirer, "How do you handle the notes as well as you do?" He replied, "I handle the notes no better than many others, but the pauses—ah! That is where the art resides."

Great presenters understand the power of the pause and use it appropriately. Pauses are especially effective when they are used to:

- Establish authority

- Emphasize important points

- Regain lost attention

- Allow time for key points to soak in

- Close the sale

When we present, we have a suspended sense of reality. To the audience, a brief pause is only a blip on the screen, but to the presenter it feels like a lifetime.

Quite often I challenge clients to experiment with pauses. After making a crucial point, I ask them to pause and count, "one-Mississippi, two-Mississippi, three-Mississippi, four-Mississippi," before moving on to their next point. After the presentation, I have them check in with their audience to see if the pause was too long. Audiences always say no.

Like any technique, pauses should be used in moderation, but when used appropriately pauses make us more powerful presenters.

Managing Nerves When Presenting

Does your voice shake or crack when you present? If so it may be because you are nervous. For some of us, speaking in public is a cause for panic.

The Power of Facing Fear

Growing up, the flying monkeys in *The Wizard of Oz* were enough to send me screaming, hiding behind the sofa in stark terror. As a child, I called a spade a spade; when I was scared, I was scared.

When I became an adult, I felt it wasn't "manly" to admit I was frightened; instead, I would say I was "stressed." Today, I recognize stress for what it is—fear.

Fear originates in a pea-sized region of the brain called the amygdala. The amygdala signals the body to prepare to either fight or flee. In this heightened state, our mouths become dry, our muscles tighten, our digestive systems shut down, and our hearts beat faster.

Psychologists tell us that one of the most effective ways to deal with fear is to recognize it for what it is, just as we did as children. Children don't ignore the fear, they engage it, and they seek to understand what is causing the fear. They also reach out to others for support. They find a parent, teacher, or trusted friend with whom they can discuss their fear and ask for advice.

In order to not be enslaved by fear, we must admit to being scared. Identifying what is triggering the fear will help us handle it better.

UCLA clinical psychologist Robert Maurer, Ph.D., believes there are only two basic fears. The first is that we aren't good enough to meet a challenge, and the second is we are going to lose control. These two fears, Maurer writes, are probably at the root of what most people call stress.

At no other time are those two fears more at play than when we present. At no other time do we feel more exposed. Courage, it's been written, is not eliminating fear but proceeding despite it. I speak to groups weekly and still get nervous. Most good speakers do. I have found that a little bit of fear is not a bad thing; it keeps me on my toes. But a lot of fear is; if not managed it can paralyze me. So the question becomes: when we experience butterflies in our stomachs before we speak, how can we get them to at least fly in formation?

Getting the Butterflies to Fly in Formation

I recently coached a young woman who became so petrified when she presented that she actually passed out once before a big presentation. Her managers were perplexed. She was one of the company's most competent professionals, but her fear of presenting was holding her back. By teaching her to focus on communicating the message and not on delivery, I was able to alleviate much of her anxiety.

Of all the tools to calm fear, none is better than changing your attitude. When you look at presentations as conversations and not performances, you begin to enjoy friendly, one-to-one conversations with individuals in the audience.

Additionally, by adopting an altruistic orientation and focusing on the audience rather than on your performance, you can transform fear into positive energy. When you're fearful, your body automatically takes a "flight or fight" stance and produces adrenaline. By directing this energy into one-on-one conversations with members of the audience, you can increase intensity, stimulate connection, and engage audiences.

You can also quiet your fear through rational thinking, positive mind talk, visualization, acting "as if," and breathing deeply through your belly.

Rational Thinking: I read once that anxiety is like fog: it is nonspecific. When you are able to name your anxiety, anxiety turns to fear, and it is more manageable.

When you look at your fears rationally, you find that most fears are future-based; they are based upon the possibility that something *may* happen, and in my experience, most of these "projected disasters" never occur.

Sometimes the worst does happen. "My biggest fear has always been that I will get a 'brain freeze' in the middle of an important speech and forget my next point," one client shared. "And then it happened. In the middle of my speech I forgot my next thought. I stopped, looked down at my notes, and found my place. It seemed like an eternity, but when I looked up at the audience I saw that they were with me. From then on, I knew I would be all right."

This strategy can work for us all. Think of the worst thing that can happen when you present. In most cases, you'll realize it's not so bad, and even if it were to happen you'd survive. I used to be so dependent on my notes that my worst fear was that I would forget them. Several years ago, I realized that if I did leave them at home I would be fine. I know this material so well that I no longer need them.

Positive Mind Talk: When you use positive mind talk, you want to employ positive wording. For example, instead of saying to yourself, "I am not afraid," you might say, "I am calm and collected." Your mind will register "calm" and "collected" instead of the negative word "afraid."

When I became more aware of the ongoing conversation in my mind, I discovered one voice that was especially harmful. My inner critic, the voice of doom, constantly whispered that I was not good enough, I wasn't lovable, and I was going to fail. His ominous warnings of woe threatened to rain havoc on every parade and every presentation.

Once conscious of this destructive force, I could dialog with it. When he hissed that I was going to embarrass myself before a big presentation, I could calmly reply, "Not likely, old man. I know my stuff." Over time, my resolution took root and my inner critic began to lose his power over me.

Visualization: In your mind's eye, you see a movie of your own making. You are the star as you successfully complete a task. You can even go beyond "seeing" your success, bringing in your other senses, too.

Before I present, I visualize the end of the presentation. I see people in the audience nodding their heads in agreement. But I also *hear* their loud applause and *feel* their approval. With renewed confidence, I am ready to speak.

Acting As If: Acting "as if" can positively shift our expectations. Many life coaches suggest that clients act as if they already have the knowledge, courage, love, and support they desire. By dressing, moving, and thinking like a strong presenter you can manifest those qualities in yourself.

Belly Breathing: Finally, belly breathing is one of the best tools for managing fear. Respiration is the body's accelerator. Studies show that many people hold their breath when they are frightened or anxious. First, remember to breathe and then slow your breathing. By slowing your breathing, your nerves are calmed.

To calm my anxiety, I use belly breathing. Specifically, I:

- Stand up straight, and let my shoulders drop, releasing all tension in the neck and shoulders.

- Let my belly and butt go. Allow the belly to be full and soft and release the butt muscles. (This is especially hard for me; I have trained myself to hold my stomach in.)

- Relax my knees so that they are neither bent nor locked.

- Plant both feet on the ground. Feel the ground on the soles of my feet.

- Breathe into my lower belly.

- Let the inhale gently roll into the exhale with a pause before the next inhale. After the exhale, I wait for the impulse to breathe in again.

I find also find "4-2-8" (mnemonic: "fortunate") especially helpful in calming nerves:

- Breathe in slowly to the count of *four*.

- Hold your breath for a count of *two*.

- Then breathe out for a count of *eight*.

More Fear-Reducing Tools

Other methods for managing presentation anxiety include:

- Get plenty of sleep the night before you present. Limit caffeine and sugar.

- Get to the room early. Familiarize yourself with the room. Meet as many of the audience members as possible before you present.

76

- Find the friendliest face in the room, or a nice "juicy face," and begin your speech looking at him or her.

- Trust in your unique presentation style. No one can play the role of you better than you.

All the tips in the world, however, won't help you reduce anxiety if you haven't prepared. Preparation is the single most effective antidote for presentation anxiety.

You now have a toolbox full of tools to help you with the fear of speaking. I have found that each person is different in terms of which tools work best for him or her. Review the above list and find the three tools you think would be most helpful to you.

Notes Are A-Okay

For many presenters—including myself—notes provide a security blanket that eases anxiety. Some say taking notes to the podium is a crutch, but I say if notes help you feel more comfortable and stay on track, use them…but use them correctly.

When not using the notes feature of PowerPoint, I counsel clients to write out their speech and then reduce it to a simple outline. This outline becomes their only notes.

Some experts advise speakers to use three-by-five-inch note cards for presentations under fifteen minutes. The cards are less noticeable than sheets of paper and draw less attention to their hands if they shake when they are nervous.

When speeches are longer than fifteen minutes, standard size sheets of paper work well. I suggest using eighteen-point type to ensure readability.

For both cards and standard paper, Melody Templeton and Suzanne Sparks Fitzgerald provide these tips in their book *Schaum's Quick Guide to Great Presentations*:

- Use only key words; use as few cards as possible.

- Use only one side.

- Number all pages (to avoid a disaster if you drop your notes).

- Include transitional phrases in your notes.

- Bring an extra copy.

How we use our notes is as important as the way we format them. Here are three suggestions for using notes:

One: Carry your notes to the podium. If you are using cards, place those cards in one hand inconspicuously. If using sheets, place them in a folder with pockets and carry the folder.

Two: Do not hold notes when you speak. When possible place them on a small table or on the lectern. In fact, you should never hold anything in your hands when you speak; it's distracting.

Three: When you have finished one thought and need to check your notes for your next thought, finish that thought with confidence, pause, look at your notes and find the next point; then reestablish eye contact with a member of the audience, and begin speaking. Take all the time you need to read your notes. Don't be afraid of the silence. As we learned earlier, pauses can be powerful.

Notes when formatted and used correctly help speakers stay on point, find their way home if they get lost, and provide a security blanket for the nervous speaker.

Speaking from a Script and Using Teleprompters
I hate scripted speeches, but some clients insist on them. If you must work off a scripted speech, here are some suggestions:

1. Above all, avoid reading the script.

2. Write the script for the ear and not the eye. Be conversational, especially at the beginning.

3. Use short, punchy phrases.

4. Pause between lines.

5. Look down. Scoop up the sentence. Reestablish eye contact with the audience and deliver the phrase. Pause a beat, then repeat.

6. Use an index finger to keep your place.

7. Use off-white, matte-finish, porous paper to avoid a reflection.

8. Place your copy on the upper two-thirds of the page, double space between lines and leave six spaces between paragraphs. Leave wide right and left margins to isolate copy in the middle of the page. Enlarge the type size, and make sure ideas and sentences end on each page.

9. Number pages.

10. Don't flip pages. Slide each page to the side, face-up.

If you haven't already, some time in your career you may have to use a teleprompter. Teleprompters are like electronic cue cards. When used properly, they help speakers connect with audiences. Speakers appear to be looking directly into the camera communicating, even though they are reading a script.

While I don't have a lot of personal experience with teleprompters, I have done a great deal of research. The most important thing to remember is that like any presentation there is no substitute for rehearsal. Practice enables you to internalize content and put more meaning into words; as a result, you will sound more natural.

Practice delivering your presentation out loud. Sometimes a sentence will read fine on paper, but must be changed for optimum vocal delivery. Practicing out loud also helps determine appropriate:

- Cadence (Break sentences into natural segments.)

- Pauses to emphasize key points

- Pronunciation

Request at least one rehearsal reading with the teleprompter to familiarize the operator with your voice and pace. Read from the upper third of the screen. You control the speed. If you have doubts, during rehearsal speed up or slow down to observe how the operator adjusts to your pace. The operator is trained to follow your pace, scrolling forward as you read. In other words, if you slow down, the screen slows down. If you speed up, the technician adjusts the screen accordingly.

One excellent way to learn how to use a teleprompter is to observe the experts. Watch television news anchors' facial expressions, head and body movements. Listen to their cadence, rhythm, and pauses. Notice the way they maintain eye contact with the camera. You may notice the left-to-right movements of their eyes as they read from a tele-prompter. Movement can be minimized by setting the screen farther away, yet not so far as to diminish readability and change the camera angle.

Remember, the teleprompter is only an aid. Your communications will not be effective if you appear to be reading. Focus on the message, not the words. You must understand the content to bring the text alive and demonstrate passion about what you're saying.

Use pitch, pace, emphasis, and pauses to make statements more conversational. Do not rush and remember to breathe. To add interest, pump energy into your delivery, but don't confuse energy with volume; this is especially critical with a taped performance.

Imagine you are looking into a friend's eyes and speak directly to him or her. This enhances your connection with the audience. It is also important to maintain eye contact with the teleprompter throughout your speech.

I worked with one client whose eyes darted periodically to the left and away from the teleprompter. It was distracting and made him look "shifty." The next time he used a teleprompter, he overcorrected; he looked like a "deer in headlights." The third time was a charm. He remembered to maintain eye contact, blink, and smile. He looked natural and was able to connect with his audience.

Remember to relax your shoulders and let the director guide your use of hand gestures. If the camera is focused on your head and shoulders, hand gestures may lead to inappropriate body movement. If a vertical shot is used, gesturing with your hands can be an excellent supplement to your delivery. While you don't want to appear rigid, don't shift positions during taping. Like any presentation, it's good to lean forward for emphasis.

Because you're relying on technology—with the potential to malfunction—bring a hard copy of your script to the video shoot.

When the director says "action," take a deep breath, wait one or two seconds, look directly into the teleprompter and begin. You are in control until the director says "cut." When you finish reading, maintain eye contact with the camera until the director says "cut."

The Power of Vulnerability

Great presenters seek connection over perfection. Connection is crucial for communication to take place, and few of us can connect, or identify, with someone who appears perfect. Perfection is rarely reality, and we seek out people who are real.

Most of the executives I coach falsely believe their presentations must be perfect. They put tremendous pressure on themselves to say the right words, the right way, at the right time, all the time. Under this kind of pressure, it's no surprise that many of them would rather eat glass than present in public.

Think back to a recent conversation you had with a friend. You probably can't remember the exact words he or she used but you can remember the point he or she wanted to make. As we have learned, effective communication is far more than the words we use.

Great presenters focus on their audiences and not on a script. Remember that our words—the actual words we use—account for only 7 percent of our credibility as a speaker. Visual and vocal cues make up the remaining 93 percent.

When we strive to be "word perfect," we do ourselves a disservice. We appear scripted and stilted because we are not our natural, authentic selves.

Quite often I work with presenters who have had a good bit of training, and in some cases this training works against them. They appear too slick and come across phony and untrustworthy.

One executive with whom I worked was so confident in his speaking abilities that he couldn't wait to present to me. After he delivered his talk, I was speechless. He was awful, and he didn't know it.

He was acting, not speaking. Audiences saw the actor but not the person behind the mask. I suggested that he begin his speech with a personal story. As he shared his story, his speech slowly came alive. We saw the speaker as a person, and the executive learned the difference between performing and presenting, between entertaining and communicating.

If you stumble and lose your place, you do not have to lose your credibility. You can simply acknowledge that you've lost your place and take a few seconds to find it. If you misquote a figure or statistic, you simply correct yourself. Most audiences won't think twice about the correction. If you don't know the answer to a hard question, you say so, but promise to find out the answer and get back to the questioner. Audiences will appreciate your honesty and responsiveness. Most audiences want you to succeed as a speaker. The last thing they want is for you to embarrass yourself because most are picturing themselves in your shoes.

Don't Sweat It

Most of us are unaware of what we give off when we communicate. When I conduct presentation training, I ask participants to present for five minutes, and then in a supportive, small group setting we give presenters feedback. In almost every case, the speaker feels he did far worse than his classmates.

"I used too many umms and ahhhs," one may say. Or another, "My voice shook; I was so nervous." But when they check in with their peers they are shocked to find out that these minor imperfections were unnoticeable.

Audiences may not expect perfection, but they do demand humanity. They want to connect with the speaker above all else. They want to get to know you; they want to know that you can be trusted. Showing them your vulnerability accomplishes these important tasks.

You can be competent and not perfect. Competence comes from knowing your stuff, and many times you learn your stuff from the mistakes you make. One of my more effective speeches was entitled, "Confessions of a Reformed Manager." In it, I recounted ten miserable mistakes I had made as a new manager. The audience of new managers was mesmerized during the hour-long presentation for they felt a real affinity with me. By exposing my flaws, I had invited them into my home. By sharing my humanity, we could walk on common ground.

Remember that great speakers combine competence with vulnerability. They seek connection over perfection. They know their stuff and are not afraid to show us who they are.

Soak in the Support

Most audiences want you to succeed. When you get up to speak almost everyone is offering you some degree of support and goodwill. When you don't pause before you speak and take in this support, you risk breaking an important connection with your audience. It's as if you have refused a well-intended gift.

If you stand still for at least one deep breath and picture yourself breathing in this support, you let your audience know that you see them and are willing to listen. What audiences crave most is to be fully seen and heard.

By taking a moment in silence you also ground yourself, giving added credibility and authority to your words. Finally, if you tend to speak fast, these few seconds in silence will help you start out at a slower, more measured pace.

At the beginning of your next talk, I challenge you to try it. Be still. Be silent, and be receptive. Soak in the audience's support.

Power Surges

- Within four seconds we form an impression of someone we just met, and he or she does the same with us.

- Fifty-five percent of our credibility as a presenter is based upon visual cues. When we present, five of these cues are particularly important:

  1. Dress and grooming

  2. Stance

  3. Eye contact

4. Gestures

5. Movement

- Think of your clothes as a communications choice. What do you want your clothes to say about you?

- Always dress one step up from your audience.

- Look in the mirror before you present. If anything stands out such as a loud tie or scarf, take it off or change it. You want the attention on your face.

- Stand tall, feet shoulder-width and pointed outward, with your weight equally distributed.

- Remember to practice one thought per person.

- Guard against those gestures that may cause you to leak authority. They include:

    o   Choir Boy or Girl

    o   Happy Pockets

    o   Firing Squad or Wooden Soldier

    o   Fig Leaf

    o   Bear Hug

    o   Lady Macbeth

- Make sure your facial expression matches your message and don't forget to smile.

- Don't hide behind a podium, chair, or table. When possible, stand where the audience can see all of you.

- Limit movement such as pacing, especially at the beginning and ending of your presentation.

- Thirty-eight percent of your credibility as a speaker is based upon the quality of your voice. Watch out for these common culprits:

    o   Rapid-fire Fiona

    o   Monotone Mike

- o   Up-talking Tina

- o   Verbal Junk Jim

- o   Breathless Brenda

- o   Cracklin' Rosie

- Remember the power of the pause.

- There are many tips for managing fear when presenting. One of the best is to think of presentations as conversations rather than performances. Others include rational thinking, positive mind talk, visualization, acting "as if," and "belly breathing."

- Remember, most audiences are on your side. They want you to succeed.

- Avoid working from a prepared script or reading slides. Notes are fine as long as they are used correctly.

- If you are using a teleprompter, remember to maintain steady eye contact with the machine. Visualize someone you know and like, and speak to them. But above all, schedule time to practice.

- Great presenters seek connection over perfection. Few of us can connect with someone who appears perfect. Audiences don't demand perfection, but they do demand humanity.

SECTION 3

GETTING AUDIENCES TO LISTEN

Chapter 4—Five Presentation Strategies

So far you've learned how to put a presentation together and how to deliver it. Now we're going to discuss how to gain mind share or how to garner attention from almost any audience. We'll review five presentation strategies: lead, listen, focus, illustrate and simplify, highlight and repeat.

To lead means to present with competence, confidence, and conviction. It means you're the ringmaster of the presentation; it's up to you to keep the presentation on track and on time. As the ringmaster, you must listen to the audience, checking in throughout the presentation to ensure you're meeting their expectations and they are agreeing with your recommendations. You also focus on the needs of the audience and bring the presentation alive by offering case studies, stories, or personal anecdotes. Finally, by simplifying, highlighting, and repeating you ensure that your message is memorable.

Presentation Strategy One: Lead

The first step to leading is getting in the right frame of mind. Do you remember the four questions on how to stand in your power in Chapter One? They were:

1. Why am I qualified to present this topic?

2. Why am I (how can I be) passionate about this topic?

3. Why should the audience care?

4. What action do I want them to take?

Asking yourself these four questions will help you establish authority as the ringmaster. Next, as ringmaster you must be the master of the clock. In those rare situations when you have all of the time you need, this isn't a problem. But what about those times when your time gets suddenly cut? For example, let's say you were scheduled to present for twenty minutes and through no fault of your own, you find yourself with only five or ten minutes.

The best approach to this challenging circumstance is what I call "the watch trick." I may say, "I understand we now have five minutes. Is that correct?" Once the group confirms the amount of time we have, I take off my watch, place it on the table, and say, "I will be respectful of your time." When I do this, the audience—especially the Samuel C. Sensors and Theodore Thinkers who may be more time sensitive—relax and can focus on our message.

Another approach is to remain other-focused and let your audience decide what you'll cover in the allotted time. "Okay, we have only ten minutes," I might say. "I was planning on talking about topic A, topic B, and topic C. Tell me what's most important to you."

Finally, as the master of the clock, your job is to keep the presentation flowing. As we discussed earlier, if audience members get stuck on a topic, you can always say, "In the interest of time, I am going to move us along."

Presentation Strategy Two: Listen, or the 70-30 Rule

Great communicators are great listeners, and they listen intently when they present. Here, I recommend what I call the "70-30 Rule." On the initial call to the prospect, at least 70 percent of your time should be spent listening. You can't sell your self, product, or company until you thoroughly understand the prospect's need. During the presentation, swap the percentages. At least 30 percent of your time should be spent listening and 70 percent should be spent presenting. I have found the more time I spend listening, the better chance I have of getting the business.

Actively listening involves asking about their expectations, inviting their questions throughout the presentation, and checking in and getting agreement during the entire process. To gain agreement, I ask such questions as:

"Does that makes sense?" (My favorite)

"Does that track with your experience?"

"Do you see how this could work for you?"

It also means listening with our eyes as well as our ears. Specific suggestions include:

- Watch to see how the audience is reacting to your pace. In many cases, you'll find you need to slow down to allow audiences to keep up with you. Remember, most salespersons sell faster than customers are willing to buy.

- Pause after each major thought and check in with your eyes with a member of the audience. Did she or he understand and/or agree with what you had to say?

- Look to see if someone disagrees or looks puzzled. If he or she does, stop and ask what is going on. The person is communicating with you with his or her facial expressions. Let the person know that he or she was heard.

- Guard against excessive noise or movement. If you hear or see it, chances are you have lost them. Regroup and focus on their needs to reengage them.

Presentation Strategy Three: Focus

The next strategy is focus. Earlier you read about the importance of focusing on the needs of your audience members. Remember to eliminate whatever doesn't do this from your presentation. Also focus on each person to whom you are presenting.

Someone asked Queen Victoria once whether she preferred the company of Benjamin Disraeli or William Gladstone. She answered that when she dined with Gladstone she felt he was the most interesting man in England, but when she ate with Disraeli she felt she was the most interesting person in the world.

Like Disraeli, we can put our egos aside and focus on the other person. We can make a conscious effort to put others' wants and needs before our own, and one way we can do it is to help people feel good about themselves. Perhaps the best way to accomplish this is to actually like the person. Earlier we discussed that "I like them" was the

Notes on Body Language

Listen with Your Eyes

If you listen only with your ears, you're missing out on much of the message. Good listeners listen with their eyes as well as their ears.

Look for feelings. The face is an eloquent communication medium. Learn to read its messages. Some nonverbal signals to watch for include:

Rubbing one eye. When you hear "I guess you're right," and the speaker is rubbing one eye, guess again. Rubbing one eye is often a signal that the speaker is having trouble inwardly accepting something.

Tapping feet. When a statement is accompanied by foot-tapping, it usually indicates a lack of confidence in what is being said.

Rubbing fingers. When you see the thumb and forefinger rubbing together, it often means that the speaker is holding something back.

Staring and blinking. If you've made your best offer and the other person stares at the ceiling and blinks rapidly, your offer is under consideration.

Crooked smiles. Most genuine smiles are symmetrical. And most facial expressions are fleeting. If a smile is noticeably crooked, you're probably looking at a fake smile.

Eyes that avoid contact. Poor eye contact can be a sign of low self-esteem, but it can also indicate that the speaker is not being truthful.

These are broad generalities; it would be unwise to make a decision based solely on these visible signals. But they can provide valuable clues. Investigate further to get an accurate picture.

number one reason why one firm is selected over another, and we tend to like people who like us. I suggest that clients find something—anything—they can like about a person.

Sometimes this is easier said than done. Face it: some people are more likeable than others. Begin by looking at people with empathy, and giving everyone the benefit of the doubt. I once worked with a man who was a real S.O.B. Sorry, but there's no other way to put it. He carried a gigantic chip on his shoulder. As I got to know him, I found out that he had never completed college. Even though he was highly successful he felt "less than" most of his peers. Once I learned this, I could be more empathetic. As I warmed to him, he warmed to me, and eventually he became one of my favorite clients.

F. Scott Fitzgerald is reported to have once said that the greatest gift you can give anyone is to see him or her exactly as he wishes to be seen. One way to help people feel seen is to remember their names.

Great presenters also remember names and other details most of us are quick to forget. Keep notes if your memory is like a sieve, like mine. Top salespeople maintain customer files for a reason. By referring to their files, they are able to refresh their memories and demonstrate a personal interest in their clients' lives.

Presentation Strategy Four: Illustrate

Nine out of ten times, when we hear a great sermon or a motivational speech, we remember the story before remembering the minister's or speaker's point. Great presenters are great storytellers. For those of us who are Samuel C. Sensors and Theodore Thinkers, storytelling may be challenging. If you find storytelling difficult, I suggest creating an inventory of stories you feel comfortable recounting, ones that drive home key points. One client—a Samuel C. Sensor—will literally ask herself before writing each presentation, "What's the story?" It's a strategy that works for her. "The last couple of presentations have been terrific," she reported. "I recently got several compliments on how engaging I was. And all I did differently was include several stories in my presentations."

Great presentations include case studies and examples, and some of the best presentations feature personal stories that offer people a glimpse of who the speaker is.

Seminar participants often ask me about humor. "It depends on whether you're funny or not," I reply. Never strain to be funny. Humor should always be natural. And it can be risky depending on the audience. Calculate if the risk is worth the benefit.

Presentation Strategy Five: Simplify, Highlight, and Repeat

The final strategy is that of constantly simplifying, highlighting, and repeating your main points.

Simplify: Be brief and to the point

Clients often retain me for presentation training when what they really want is help organizing their thoughts. I hear them say things like:

"My boss says that I take too long to get the point."

"I have trouble articulating what I really mean."

"I don't seem to hold my audience's attention."

Forbes Magazine estimates that most speeches last forty minutes. Ron Huff in his book *Say It in Six* says six minutes or shorter is the ideal length for any communication. While it may be impossible to restrict every communication to six minutes, I would agree—brevity is best.

Brevity often accompanies greatness. Consider:

- When Nelson Mandela was released from prison in South Africa, he made a stunning speech that marked the end of apartheid. The entire speech lasted only five minutes.

- Winston Churchill's "Never Give In" speech lasted six minutes and "Blood, Toil, Tears, and Sweat" was even shorter, two and a half minutes.

- Susan B. Anthony made one of the strongest speeches ever for woman's rights, over a hundred years ago, in less than five minutes.

Huff offers a five-step worksheet to "say it in six."

1. "Let's get right to the point. There's a burning issue here that we need to discuss…"

2. "Here's a quick overview—just a bit of background…"

3. "This led to an idea…"

4. "This idea will more than pay for itself. Here's the payoff…"

5. "Here's what we need from you to get going…"

I recommend that clients structure their thoughts by answering these questions:

1. What is the one message, mission, or theme you want to communicate?

2. What are the sub-themes that fall under the central theme (can you limit them to three)?

3. What case studies, examples, or personal stories bring life to these sub-themes?

4. What action do you want your audience to take?

5. What is the benefit to them for taking this action?

Brevity means short, not shallow. By structuring your presentations around these five questions, you'll streamline your communications, maintain audiences' attention, and motivate them to action.

Highlight: Use flagging phrases
While some politicians don't have a reputation for being authentic communicators, many are masters in how to hold audiences' attention. These politicians know how to use "flagging phrases."

When Richard Nixon said, "Let me make myself perfectly clear," the world stopped and took note, and when George H. W. Bush told us, "Read my lips," we hung on every word. These phrases are what public relations professionals call "flagging phrases," and they have the same effect as tapping a spoon to a glass at a banquet; everyone stops to tune into what the speaker has to say. When you use these phrases in talks and presentations, audience members pick up their pens and write down what follows. Flagging phrases break through the clutter and increase the audience's mindshare.

One of the most effective ways to flag audiences' attention is to use numbers. When you say, "There are *'x'* points to remember" listeners become alert and ready to record each point.

By encouraging audiences to tune into station WIIFT (What's In It For Them), we can also flag their attention. Common WIIFT phrases include:

- "What this means to you...."
- "That's an important point because...."
- "You may be interested to know...."

Still another flagging phrase is to end our talk by saying, "In summary" or "In conclusion." Most audiences tune back into the speaker when he or she recaps the important points at the end of a speech.

There are many other flagging phrases. Some of my favorites are:

- "Please don't forget...."
- "The best part about...."
- "The key is...."
- "The fact is...."
- "The most important thing is...."
- "The bottom line is...."

Which of these phrases do you like? Add them to your communications toolbox and try them out during your next presentation.

Repeat: The Rule of Three
Your mama may have told you not to repeat yourself, but I say don't forget the Rule of Three: (1) tell them what you're going to tell them, (2) tell them, and (3) tell them what you told them.

For Women Only

Many of my clients are women. I have found that most women are damned-if-they-do and damned-if-they-don't when it comes to communicating in the male-dominated worlds of politics, business, and education. In order to compete, they must find a delicate balance between authority and likeability.

All great communicators possess what I call "the terrific triad," credibility, likeability, and authority. While many women want to claim their authority, they are concerned about appearing too domineering or abrasive, and thus losing likeability. "We are in a double bind," one female executive shared.

To make matters worse, our culture associates authority with men. When we think of those traits we consider authoritative, we immediately think of tall, solidly built, and having a lower-pitched voice—all characteristics associated with men, not women.

In today's world, women are expected to be both authoritative and feminine. Most women agree that's difficult.

In my years as a communications trainer and coach, I've learned that most women have to sacrifice some likeability for authority, and that is okay.

Many women naturally have high likeability factors and can ramp up their authority and not lose all their likeability. Here are five of their secrets:

One: Go for it. Don't wait for an invitation or permission, and interrupt if you must. Former Secretary of State Madeline Albright is reported to have said that learning to interrupt is one of the most important things a young woman must learn.

Two: Get to the point, and stay on point. Business speak—like most men's conversational styles—is linear. Be succinct; avoid personal stories and too much detail. Be honest and direct without being unfriendly. Minimize feeling words and substitute facts.

Three: Mirror their style. Turn up the volume, and lower the pitch. Maintain steady eye contact; don't nod your head or cock it to the side. Don't smile excessively or fidget. "Own" the space on which you stand or sit.

Four: Avoid disclaimers. Avoids "buts," self put-downs, unwarranted apologies, excuses, or upward intonations. Top management values confidence and conviction above all else.

Five: Remain flexible. "…female leadership characteristics, once a hindrance to success, are being accepted as valuable business skills that are imperative in a changing, diverse, and competitive workplace," writes Susan Wilson Solovic in *The Girl's Guide to Power and Success*. Some situations call for a "command and control" male communications strategy, but others require a "softer" female approach that is more collaborative.

Women are not the only gender being called upon to flex their communications style in business today. More and more businessmen are seeing that a collaborative communications style works better in some business situations: for example, recruiting and retaining the brightest talent, and creating and maintaining strategic business partnerships. And as women gain more power, men are finding that they have no choice but to adapt their styles to match those of women. While gender plays a role in communication, nothing is as important as authenticity.

Back to Authenticity

The sharpest tool in a PowerHouse Presenter's toolbox is authenticity. Let me illustrate. I had been called by a company to help a rising star from becoming a falling one. His presentation skills were holding him back.

When I called his manager for feedback, she offered these observations: "When he presents he is a wreck, but when you talk with him one-on-one he instills confidence. It's as if he's two different people." I asked her to continue. "When he presents, he fidgets and doesn't seem to know what to do with his hands. He uses a lot of umms and ahs and reads the slides. I am a nervous wreck by the time he sits down," she continued.

My rising star had adopted a performance orientation to presenting. He had forgotten a basic truth about presenting: All communications is one-on-one whether talking to one person or presenting to one thousand. I suggested that he delete the word "presenting" from his vocabulary and substitute it with the word "communicating." I also suggested that he share a little more of himself with people.

A definite introvert, he was reluctant to share his true self with a group. Instead, he hid behind the material and spoke to the room and not to individuals in the room. I helped him see that communications is not about performing but connecting. And self-disclosure plays a critical role in forming strong connections with people.

I read once that who we are speaks much louder than what we have to say, for what really sells people on anything is the authenticity of the presenter. The more comfortable we are, the more compelling we become. Great presenters are real. They speak with conviction, clarity, and with the intention of connecting.

Terry Pearce in his book *Leading Out Load: The Authentic Speaker, The Credible Leader* writes that in order to speak authentically, a presenter must have conviction or passion for his or her cause and be able to communicate it clearly in a way that connects with the audience.

Audiences connect with speakers who prove their competence while showing their vulnerability. And audiences are more likely to follow the directive of those speakers when they speak with conviction that mixes passion with reason.

In summary, five keys will help make you and your presentations more authentic and credible:

1. Trust in your own communications style. No one can play you better than you.

2. Make it personal for you and for your audience; include feelings as well as facts, and tell personal stories.

3. Speak from conviction; connect with your passion.

4. Be sincere; say it only if you mean it.

5. Acknowledge the challenges, including resistance, uncertainty, and your own vulnerability.

Our world is starved for truly competent, trustworthy leadership. Speaking is a vital part of that leadership, and its true power comes from conviction, clarity, and connection.

"Leaders can no longer simply stand in front of a room and tell people what to do," writes Lee Glickstein in his book *Be Heard Now! Tap Into Your Inner Speaker and Communicate with Ease*. "To make an impact, we need to forge a strong, heartfelt relationship with people. That means we have to be authentic and human with them. We have to let them in, so that they will let our message in."

Power Surges

- Five presentation strategies will help you get audiences to listen to you:

  1. Lead

  2. Listen

  3. Focus

  4. Illustrate

  5. Simplify, highlight, and repeat

- To lead you must be a "master of the clock." Keep the presentation moving while adapting to the audience's needs.

- Remember the 70-30 Rule. During the initial call on the prospect at least 70 percent of your time should be spent listening. During the presentation, at least 30 percent should be spent engaging and listening to your audience.

- Remember to listen with your eyes as well as your ears. Don't move on with the presentation until you have received confirmation from the audience that they are with you.

- Remember to be "other focused" by focusing on the needs of your audience.

- Present one thought to a person as if he or she was the only person in the room.

- Great presenters are great storytellers.

- Use numbers to get on point and stay on point.

- Use "flagging phrases" to command attention.

- In order to compete, women must find a delicate balance between likeability and authority. Most woman have naturally high likeability factors; their challenge is to ramp up authority. Five suggestions:

  1. Speak out; interrupt if you must.

  2. Get on point and stay on point.

  3. Mirror a masculine style by turning up the volume, lowering the pitch, and maintaining steady eye contact. Own the space where you stand.

  4. Avoid disclaimers.

  5. Remain flexible between a masculine and feminine communications style.

- Above all, audiences are attracted to authenticity. Five keys will help make you and your presentations more authentic and credible:

  1. Trust in your own communications style. No one can play you better than you.

  2. Make it personal for you and your audience; include feelings as well as facts and tell personal stories.

  3. Speak from conviction; connect with your passion.

  4. Be sincere; say it only if you mean it.

  5. Acknowledge the difficult stuff; include resistance, uncertainty, and your own vulnerability.

Conclusion

Several years ago, I received an e-mail from a former client. Her son is in the fourth grade at Groveland Elementary School in Minnetonka, Minnesota. Each fall the school has a "demonstration project" in which the students are asked to give a five- to ten-minute presentation on something they have researched. Past demonstrations have included everything from candle making to card tricks.

When she arrived an hour early to see her son's presentation, his teacher put her to work coaching the anxious students. As expected she saw lots of ducked heads, mumbling, and glassy-eyed recitation. In her e-mail to me, she wrote, "I couldn't take it any longer. I gathered the class and told them about your seminar. I explained that whether speaking to one person or to one hundred, communication is all the same, and that they didn't have to be any different *up there* than they were here. I told them, 'If you don't remember anything else I've said, remember to stand in your power.'"

For the next three days of presentations, the teacher told each child, "Stand in your power!" before he or she began to speak. The words resonated so deeply with these kids that the teachers printed "Stand in Your Power!" on posters and placed them in each classroom.

My client concluded, "So thanks from the teachers and me. And thanks from my son, who thinks he's pretty hot stuff now that he's taught thirty kids how to make toffee."

If fourth graders can become PowerHouse Presenters, you can too. The key to doing so is to remember to "stand in your power."

When you stand in your power, you are comfortable enough with yourself to unflinchingly share all that you are. You strive to let audiences know you by being yourself and sharing your life. You communicate in the same manner regardless of the number of people to whom you are speaking. Whether having a casual conversation over coffee with a friend or speaking in front of a hundred strangers, you speak in the same relaxed manner. Finally, you place your focus not on your performance but on connecting with people, meeting their needs, and clearly communicating your point.

So the next time you speak to a group, remember—along with the fourth graders of Groveland Elementary School—to stand in your power!

One Last Word

Wow, we're covered a lot of information in a short amount of space. Now may be a good time to recap. You first learned the four homework assignments that you must complete before beginning any proposal. They were: know your audience, know your venue, select your visuals, and get in the right frame of mind. You met Samuel C. Sensor, Theodore Thinker, Ina Intuitor, and Felicia Feeler and learned the importance of flexing your style to match that of others, especially the decision maker. You also learned the psychology of presenting. You discovered that great speakers work from the inside out by first getting in the right frame of mind. And at the end of the chapter, we reviewed the five basic truths about communications:

1. All communication is one on one.

2. All communication is two-way.

3. All communication is "other" focused.

4. People respond most to your intentions, especially how you feel about them.

5. People respond less to the actual words you use than to the way you present yourself, particularly visual and vocal cues.

In Chapter Two, we covered how to put and hold presentations together. We discussed several types of proposals or speeches, including sales presentations, speeches to inform or educate, consulting presentations, and Snap presentations. We went over tips for how to make a strong positive impression when presenting to top management. You also learned how to manage the question and answer period and what to do when audiences start to take control of the presentation.

From there we moved on to Section Two: How to Deliver a Presentation. Since 93 percent of a speaker's credibility is based on visual and vocal cues, we focused our attention there. We spent a good bit of time on how to make impressive first impressions, or open the four-second window. Under visual cues, we discussed dress, stance, eye contact, gestures, and movement. You learned how to dress and stand with authority, deliver one thought per person, gesture naturally, and limit movement when speaking. And under vocal cues, I shared common pitfalls and their antidotes. You met Rapid-fire Fiona, Tiny Tom, Monotone Mike, Up-talking Tina, Verbal Junk Jim, Breathless Brenda, and Cracklin' Rosie. You learned the power of the pause. We concluded this section with a discussion on how to manage the jitters when you speak, including how to use notes and a scripted speech properly.

In Section Three: Getting Audiences to Listen, we reviewed five presentation strategies for how to get audiences to listen and take note. They were: lead by becoming a master of the clock, listen with your eyes as well as your ears, focus your material exclusively on the audience's needs, illustrate your presentation with stories and case studies, and simplify, highlight with flagging phrases, and repeat. I gave a few tips on how to be brief and to the point for those who may be a little long-winded. I also offered several suggestions for how women can project authority since they face specific challenges when presenting. Then I concluded the section by reviewing the strongest tool in the PowerHouse Presenting toolbox, authenticity. If you don't remember anything else, remember this: the primary determinant for becoming a PowerHouse Presenter, powerful communicator, and effective leader is authenticity. By knowing, embracing, and sharing all that you are, you will become the communicator and leader you were born to be.

I hope you enjoyed Powerhouse Presenting and even experienced an "aha" or two. You may feel a little overwhelmed; we covered a lot of information. I highly recommend that you select one or two items and concentrate on implementing those in your presentations. For example, many clients begin with "one thought per person" or their stance. Once you master those, you can select two more items and work on those. And don't forget to review the Power Surges at the end of each chapter.

Please be gentle on yourself. There's an old saying in twelve-step work: "practice, not perfection." Concentrate on getting it right only in the first three minutes of the presentation when you are making that first impression.

Remember, a lot of what you learned can be practiced every day, not just when you present. When you are sitting with a group of friends around the lunch table, practice one thought per person or being totally present. Or when speaking with your boss in the hall, pay attention to how you are standing. Make sure you are standing tall, own the space, and have your weight equally distributed. Try using a flagging phrase when you want to ensure that your point is heard, and remember to use numbers to stay on point. Practice is how you'll become a PowerHouse Presenter.

In the resources section of this book, I've included some additional tools to further assist you, including a personal presentation style inventory. Ask a trusted friend or coworker to fill it out for you the next time you present. And on my website, buildyourleaders.com, you'll find numerous additional resources that you may find helpful, including information about my coaching and training services. Finally, I highly recommend that you sign up to receive my complimentary monthly eNewsletter. You'll find a sign-up box on my website. If you know of others who might also benefit from my eNewsletter, I hope you'll send them the link.

In conclusion, I hope you'll take a minute to acknowledge yourself for your willingness to undertake this journey with me. It's been both a pleasure and honor to work with you.

Randy Siegel

Randy@BuildYourLeaders.com

Resources

Several resources follow. For more information and resources on becoming the communicator you were born to be, please visit my website at buildyourleaders.com. Listings are updated regularly.

If you are asked to give a speech, you may find this checklist helpful.

Speaker's Checklist

Group:

Contact Name:

Phone Number:

Address:

Date:

Subject:

Length of Speech:

Goal:

Location/Directions:

Audience:
- Size:

- Interests/attitude/knowledge of subject:

- Sensitive issues:

- Gender/education/ethnic mix/age considerations:

- Individuals to be aware of:

Meeting:
- Format:

- Length:

- Q & A:

- Other speakers:

- Past speakers' subjects:

- Frequency of meeting:

- Purpose of meeting/mission:

- Who presides:

- Who will introduce speaker:

- Press coverage:
- Venue:
- Size:
- Seating:
- Acoustics (microphone):
- A/V equipment:
- Podium/stage:
- Lighting:

Other Notes:

Personal Presentation Style Inventory

When I conduct Powerhouse Presenting workshops, the first part of the day is spent in an interactive classroom where we cover much of the material contained in this book. In the afternoons, I coach small groups of six.

In a supportive environment, participants present in front of five of their peers. Using this form, we then conduct an inventory of what works well and what could be improved on. From there, I coach each participant, focusing on one or two areas that will give them the greatest improvement. My goal is to increase each participant's skill level by 30 percent before she or he completes the workshop.

Consider copying this form and asking several peers to help you evaluate your presentation skills. Rank each of the attributes under the five areas below one (low) through five (high).

Likeable: Would I want to work with this person? Is he/she:

___ Warm

___ Sincere/Trustworthy

___ Fun/Good Sense of Humor

___ Human/Real

1	2	3	4	5
Low				High

Credible: Does the presenter know her/his stuff? Is he/she:

___ Knowledgeable of Subject

___ Well Organized

1	2	3	4	5
Low				High

Authoritative: Is the presenter comfortable and confident? Does she/he have good:

___ Eye Contact

___ Stance

___ Natural Gestures

___ Voice Quality

1	2	3	4	5
Low				**High**

Visual: Does the presenter have a nice visual impact?

___ Dress

___ Gestures

___ Stance

___ Movement

___ Eye Contact

1	2	3	4	5
Low				**High**

Vocal: Does the presenter have good vocal quality?

___ Articulation

___ Pauses

___ Pace

___ Projection

___ Vocal Variation

___ Distraction (um, ers, you knows)

1	2	3	4	5
Low				**High**

Video and Audio Conferencing: When Presenting Is Not Face-to-Face

As more companies turn to video and audio conferencing in an effort to save time and money, more of my clients are requesting information on how to shine when presentations are not face-to-face.

When I ran the Atlanta office of an international public relations agency, I was required to participate in quarterly profit center meetings, many of which were video conferences. Since the audience was the agency's top management, my success or failure depended not only on my office's numbers, but also on the way I came across in these meetings.

Looking Your Best During a Video Conference

I quickly learned that unlike being interviewed on television, video-conferencing participants should concentrate eye contact on the camera rather than on others around the conference table or in the room. If there are multiple cameras, participants should check the television monitor lights to ensure that they are facing the camera that is currently online. While looking into the camera, I found it helpful to look *through* the camera and visualize a friendly face watching from another site.

I wear reading glasses, but I used them only when I needed them and was careful not to gesture with them. After a while, I invested in non-reflective lenses.

I found that the same rules apply to dressing for a video conference or Web cam as for a television interview:

- Stay away from high contrast colors such as black and white.

- Avoid reds; they may "bleed."

- Select pastels over white (men, consider a light blue oxford shirt).

- Don't wear patterned fabrics as they might "dance" on the screen.

- Dress simply and avoid anything that stands out such as a broach, drop earrings, or a wild tie. (Always avoid clothes or accessories that distract your audience.)

Men should select medium-dark colors for suits; navy and charcoal gray are my favorites. Since women have more options on colors for suits, skirts and dresses, they should choose those color(s) that look best on them.

Finally, it's a good idea to visit the video-conferencing room well before the meeting to ensure that your clothing doesn't clash with the room's fabrics or colors. Of course, how participants dress makes no difference in an audio or telephone conference.

Holding Audiences' Attention

Anyone who has participated in an audio or video conference knows it's harder to hold people's attention than in face-to-face meetings. Two helpful tips are:

1. Keep your presentation shorter than a typical face-to-face meeting. No speaker should speak for more than five to seven minutes.

2. Break up your presentation with graphics, interaction, reports, or video clips.

While video conferencing equipment has improved, some of it still suffers from slight audio delays. Participants should pause longer than usual to allow others to respond. Also, it is wise to wait a second or two before making a point or changing the subject to ensure that other participants have finished their comments.

> **Fact**
>
> Off camera, video conference participants and most audio conference participants multi-task during the meeting.

Video conferencing cameras tend to exaggerate gestures. In order to look authoritative and not overly aggressive, limit sudden movements such as shifting weight or crossing legs. Also eliminate sweeping gestures including pointing fingers or extending hands. Negative facial expressions and body language are especially amplified.

"Barbara" forgot my advice to act as if she was always on camera, so when "Rick" began to present a proposal with which she disagreed, she frowned in protest. After the videoconference, her boss scolded her for not being a member of the team.

Be aware of rolling cameras and open microphones. Remember you are "live." When someone else is speaking, keep an interested, friendly, and receptive expression. Assume everyone is looking at you all the time.

Also, avoid playing with your pen, eating, swiveling in your chair, or becoming too relaxed. Always use the mute button on your microphone whenever you are not speaking.

Sounding Good During an Audio Conference

Void of all visuals, the audio conference depends strictly on vocal cues. Conference participants should remember to:

- Identify themselves when they speak.

- Speak in a normal tone and volume.

- Vary their speech patterns for interest: high-low, fast-slow.

- Lower their pitch and/or increase volume to convey more authority.

- Dramatically increase or lower volume to gain attention.

- Articulate.

- Stand up in order to think clearer.

- Use the mute button when not speaking.

Once a client, "Jennifer," was "busted" for returning e-mails during an audio conference. Participants heard her typing. "Never again," she told me.

In conclusion, whether participating in a video or audio conference, treat people as participants and not as passive viewers. Let them know you know they are out there.

Do's and Don'ts of Videoconferencing

- Do:

  o Pause and look in the camera for a second or two after you speak to establish authority.

  o If you use slides, follow the tips for slides in Chapter 1.

- Don't:

  o Look at yourself in the monitor.

  o Lean too close to the microphone or your P's will pop and your S's hiss.

  o Talk too long. Talk no more than five to seven minutes. Remember, it's harder to hold the audience's attention during video conferences versus face-to-face meetings.

Webcasting

Two-thirds of home computers will have Web cams within the next two years, experts predict. To be at your communications best when Webcasting consider:

Dress: As with video conferencing, dress in muted solids. Blues, grays, and maroons work especially well. Avoid patterns, thin stripes, herringbone, or solid white.

Camera Angle: Aim the camera lens at eye level. Aimed down, you will appear lacking authority and small; aimed up, you will appear large and threatening.

Posture: Lean slightly forward to engage your viewer.

Voice: Speak as if the person was next to you.

Set: Get rid of any distractions such as clutter on your desk. Ensure good lighting and watch for shadows.

Afterword

Becoming a Great Communicator

Sometimes it's hard to remember in business that we are connected first as human beings rather than the roles we play—managers, employees, suppliers, clients, salespeople. When we communicate as our authentic selves—when we "step into our power"—we invite others to do the same. We forge strong relationships that can only benefit us in our work and personal lives.

While important, presenting is but one aspect of communications. Today's savvy businesspeople recognize the need to, and benefit of, forging stronger connections with key constituents. They understand that—to influence, motivate, and inspire—communication must entail more than the simple exchange of information. It must create a connection between sender and receiver.

Key to connection is trust. Authenticity, vision, conviction, competency, clarity, and caring convey attributes of a trustworthy person. We can communicate all six by using four tools borrowed from business, sociology, and psychology, all of which begin with the letter "P."

Personhood gives us a strong sense of self so that we aren't afraid to share our authentic selves with others. **Purpose** transforms careers into callings, ignites passion, and empowers the way in which we speak. **Persona** describes the masks we wear, or images we assume, in order to facilitate communication. In business, it is our professional image, or the way we brand ourselves professionally. Finally, **presence** is the way in which we carry ourselves and listen to others, and it determines in large part our ability to convey likeability, credibility, and authority—three hallmarks of powerful communicators.

The strongest communicators and leaders express themselves from the inside out, grounding themselves in a strong sense of self and service before speaking. Because they know communications is far more than the words we use and how we speak them, they pay rapt attention to all that they are communicating about themselves. Finally, when they do speak, they present in ways that make people want to listen.

We can picture personhood, purpose, persona, and presence as the four points of a cross that is contained within a circle. Personhood is at the bottom of the cross where it grounds the model; purpose is at the top. On the far left, is persona, and on the opposite axis is presence. It is where the four points intersect in the middle that we are at our most powerful as communicators.

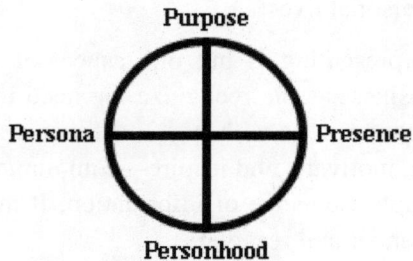

By harnessing the power of the four Ps, we can influence, motivate, and inspire others. We can:

- Successfully sell our ideas, products, services, and self

- Retain and grow existing clients

- Build consensus, facilitate problem solving, and encourage teamwork.

- Build strong relationships both at work and at home

- Live a life that matters

To learn more about this exciting process, purchase my book *Engineer Your Career: A Blueprint for Your Best Self,* available at Amazon.com or buildyourleaders.com.

www.ingramcontent.com/pod-product-compliance
Lightning Source LLC
Chambersburg PA
CBHW031946190326
41519CB00007B/683